Dr. Jensen's
JUICING
THERAPY

Dr. Jensen's
JUICING
THERAPY

NATURE'S WAY TO BETTER
HEALTH AND A LONGER LIFE

Bernard Jensen, D.C., Ph.D.
Clinical Nutritionist

New York Chicago San Francisco Lisbon London Madrid Mexico City
Milan New Delhi San Juan Seoul Singapore Sydney Toronto

The **McGraw·Hill** Companies

Library of Congress Cataloging-in-Publication Data

Jensen, Bernard, 1908–
    [Juicing therapy]
    Dr. Jensen's juicing therapy : nature's way to better health and a longer life /
Bernard Jensen.
        p.   cm.
    Includes index.
    ISBN 0-658-00279-1
    1. Fruit juices—Therapeutic use.   2. Vegetable juices—Therapeutic use.
  I. Title: Doctor Jensen's juicing therapy.   II. Title.
  RM225 .J46   2000
  615.5'35—dc21   99-89330

16 17 18 19 20 21 22 23 24 25 26   QFR/QFR   1 5 4 3 2

ISBN 978-0-658-00279-3
MHID   0-658-00279-1

McGraw-Hill books are available at special quantity discounts to use as premiums and
sales promotions, or for use in corporate training programs. For more information, please
write to the Director of Special Sales, Professional Publishing, McGraw-Hill, Two Penn
Plaza, New York, NY 10121-2298. Or contact your local bookstore.

The purpose of this book is to educate. It is sold with the understanding that the publisher
and author shall have neither liability nor responsibility for any injury caused or alleged to
be caused directly or indirectly by the information contained in this book. While every
effort has been made to ensure its accuracy, the book's contents should not be construed
as medical advice. Each person's health needs are unique. To obtain recommendations
appropriate to your particular situation, please consult a qualified health-care provider.

This book is printed on acid-free paper.

Let's drink for health!
The necessary cutting-edge therapy may be in the
fresh juices to reclaim and maintain our health.

—Dr. Bernard Jensen

CONTENTS

PREFACE

I was introduced to the healing power of juices early in my career when a thirty-year-old woman came to my office with thirteen leg ulcers, several the size of silver dollars and open with running pus. Three years of treatments by several doctors had not helped her.

She had been examined and treated at two of the top medical clinics in the United States. At one of them, she was treated for hypocalcemia, a shortage of calcium, which her doctor believed to be part of her problem. He prescribed pharmaceutical calcium, which she could not assimilate. This young woman was getting very discouraged until someone told her about my work as a clinical nutritionist.

As I listened to her story, I couldn't help but wonder how I was going to assist a person who so many other doctors had tried to help but failed. Then I thought of the elderly in Pakistan's Hunza Valley who still had every tooth in their heads, strong bones, and healthy skin at ages over a hundred years. Where did they get their calcium? Why did they have such good calcium control? It most certainly was partly due to the fresh greens they ate.

Fresh greens are high in the vitamin A precursor, carotene, which helps control calcium in the body. Greens also contain a significant amount of calcium. I thought if I could get her to drink juice from several different kinds of green vegetables, maybe it would speed up the healing of the leg ulcers. She would be getting an easily assimilated natural form of calcium in the juice, and she would also be getting enough vitamin A to control the distribution in the body.

I believe in putting my patients to work so that they are involved in their own healing processes. Day after day, I had the woman chop up green leafy vegetables—spinach, dandelion greens, kale, and I don't know how many others. We soaked them in water until all the good green juices had "bled" into the water, then strained it through cheesecloth. She drank a glass of this green vegetable juice diluted in water every hour, all day.

It was hard work, but it paid off. In three weeks, the thirteen leg ulcers were completely healed. The secret was in the juice! What prescription remedies from drugstores failed to cure, Mother Nature completely healed.

I want to bring attention to the chlorophyll in the green leafy vegetable juice because I am certain that it played an important role in the healing process, too. Chlorophyll is the lifeblood of plants and one of the most wonderful blood cleansers I have ever used with patients. It cleanses the blood by cleansing the bowel of those toxins most commonly assimilated into the bloodstream. "When you're green inside, you're clean inside," I always told my patients. Experience has demonstrated to me the value of keeping the bowel clean by means of chlorophyll-rich drinks. A clean bowel helps prevent disease.

The success of this case and hundreds like it eventually established my reputation and increased my confidence in what I was bringing into my patients' lives and bodies. I enjoy seeing people improve their health, and juices are a wonderful source of nutrients that I believe we all need to take advantage of to reach for the highest level of health and well-being we can get.

Juices (and other liquids) are the fastest method I know for getting nutrients—in easily digested and assimilated form—into the blood and lymph systems that feed the cells and maintain the body's health. We find that fruit juices tend to supply more vitamins, while vegetable juices tend to supply more minerals, although each contain both. (Juice should be used soon after being made because some vitamins and minerals are oxidized soon after extraction from their source. Also, live enzymes don't last long in juice.) Freshness and ripeness are factors that influence the nutritional value of the fruits and vegetables we run through our juicers, but soil is by far the most important influence. If the soil is depleted of important minerals, the fruit and vegetables grown from that soil will be depleted of those same minerals. The label "organic" on a fruit or vegetable doesn't guarantee that it has been grown on mineral-rich soil, so we need to do a certain amount of research and investigation to find out where the fruits and vegetables we purchase are grown and what the quality of the soil is in that place.

I want to make clear that I don't believe we can make a life on juices—we need fiber foods for bowel tone and proper elimination, including whole grains, raw nuts, and seeds, and sources of protein such as eggs, cheese, and yogurt. A juice diet is not a balanced diet, but there may be times when a juice fast is appropriate for certain physical ailments and conditions, as discussed in chapter 2.

In my own nutritional regimen, I use juices much the same as I use supplements—to get specific nutrients into the body fast so that they can get to the cells and restore proper function and balance. The vitamins, minerals, and enzymes present in juices are assimilated and launched into the bloodstream or lymph system much faster than if solid food had been eaten.

I believe in juices. I believe we can easily include a juice snack in our diets twice a day for better health and well-being and for an extra measure of protection from disease. I want to emphasize the need for variety in the kinds of juices we use because variety is the only way we can be sure of getting all the different nutrients we need every day.

If you want to feel better and live longer, juicing and juices are for you.

INTRODUCTION

This little book can bring you new life if you pay close attention to what you are reading and if you become "doers of the word, and not hearers only"! It may save you from aging before your time and may greatly reduce the amount of money you invest in your family physician.

We must learn the simple truth, that we don't (and can't) heal a disease. It is the patient we should be taking care of, not the diseases, and we take a giant step forward in our own understanding and perspective when we recognize that juices are great health builders, but they are not "medications" prescribed to alleviate or suppress disease symptoms.

Your health and life can be changed if you act on what is in this book.

Nutrition is the foundational healing art, absolutely necessary before any kind of healing can take place in the body. How can I say this? Because only the chemical elements from foods can rebuild cells or correct defects in cells, and because our ultimate source of chemical elements is foods; the success of all other healing arts depends on this one healing art.

We need to get it into our heads that foods have the chemicals needed for tissue repair. Foods, including juices, build tissue, and when a sufficient amount of cleansing and building has taken place, the body heals itself by virtue of natural laws.

Hippocrates said, "We will never understand disease until we understand foods." He meant the makeup of foods, the chemical elements needed for repair and rebuilding. He had no idea of the nutrients in foods or the chemical elements, but he knew foods played a part in preparing a patient for healing.

I have visited the island of Kos where Hippocrates was born and raised, and I paid my respects to this venerable healer who first pointed out that foods must be included in the healing process. Hippocrates said, "Foods should be your medicine, and your medicine should be your food." We need to inform ourselves about the foods available in our own corner of the world and learn what those foods can and cannot do for us.

People with seriously compromised health may have to use supplements and juices quite a lot at first, but our objective should always be to work toward a balanced regimen of whole, pure, and natural foods, as described in my Health and Harmony Food Regimen (see chapter 1). I want to note here that juices are foods, not supplements in the usual understanding of the word.

It is important for those of us who want better health to take greater responsibility for our own health. This book will explain some effective ways of doing this. We have to care about staying healthy, or else who will care for us? We find that disease can come when we don't care, when we don't have the proper foods going into our bodies, and when we are living on processed, altered foods instead of foods that are natural, pure, fresh, and whole.

Dr. V. G. Rocine was my greatest teacher, my greatest mentor. He taught me which chemical elements are in certain foods and how they are best absorbed by the body. His teachings as well as those of Hippocrates have been the principal influence of my life's work. But it's not enough simply to learn what is good for you. If you need to make juices out of foods that are high in calcium, *do it*. Find out what greens you can use, juice them, and get them into your body as soon as you can. Better health begins the day you start.

You may not feel different the next day, but a start has been made. Remember, you never felt the first instant that a problem began in your body, either. You'll never hear, feel, or see what one single salad will do for you, but if you have a salad every day for a year, you'll know it does you good. If you have juices every day for a year as a supplement to your regular foods, I believe you will be delighted at the improvement in your well-being.

I visited the isolated Hunza Valley in Pakistan many years ago to find out for myself if the people were as disease-free and long-lived as Robert McCarrison, M.D., who was influential in the founding of the organic farming movement, reported in the early part of this century. In a world that seems to be constantly on the verge of being overwhelmed by disease, the residents of the Hunza Valley were a refreshing contrast. There were no jails, hospitals, policemen, or doctors. Why? Because the people were mentally and socially healthy and well balanced. They lived in a high Himalayan valley where the compromised foods, customs, and manners of civilization could not easily reach them and where they had to live off the simple foods they grew on glacier-watered soil. Cancer, heart disease, diabetes, kidney disease, and arthritis were unknown by the residents of the Hunza while I was there. (There was a problem with goiter due to a lack of iodine in their foods, I was told later, but I didn't see any during my visit.)

The foods we eat and the lifestyle we live have a great deal of influence over our health and longevity. Some of the Hunzakuts I met were over 120 years old and still had all their teeth, smooth skin, clear eyes, and good memories, and were able to walk for miles to work in the fields or visit friends and relatives. The Hunza diet was high in natural carbohydrates and low in protein. They walked up and down steep mountain roads and trails every day. I didn't see anyone overweight because the meals were generally sparse, although rich in nutritional value.

It is possible for us to learn from and imitate parts of the Hunza lifestyle for longer life and better health. Naturally, juices should be an everyday part of our program. A lot of minerals are locked up in vegetables and fruits, and juicing releases them. Juices are one of the great ways of getting these minerals back into our bodies.

It is my responsibility, however, to urge you to be cautious about juices and use your head about how much to consume. I don't think you should go off and live for sixty days on carrot juice or forty-five days on orange juice. Any juice fast should be discussed with and possibly overseen by your doctor. Always discuss any unique health regimen or drastic diet change with your doctor before you consider acting on it.

Juicing is an unconventional therapy that saturates the body's tissues with vitamins, minerals, and enzymes, enabling tissue to throw off encumbrances in good time. It can strengthen the body to begin reversing a disease.

One of the ways we know that diet makes a significant impact on our health and longevity is because studies have been done on the Seventh-Day Adventists, a Christian denomination committed to a largely vegetarian diet. The overwhelming majority do not use alcohol, tobacco, or drugs. They have almost no incidence of lung cancer, and their statistics on cancer, in general, and heart disease show they have much less of these killer diseases than other Americans. In fact, they seem to have less trouble with all diseases than does the general population. They use a balanced approach to diet.

I met an old man in the Caucasus Mountains of the former USSR whose name was Gassanoff. He was 153 years of age. They put us on public television in Moscow, and I asked him, "What rules have you used for living 153 years?" He said, "I didn't even know I was going to live 153 years. I have no rules." Nevertheless, his lifestyle and diet of simple, nutritious foods were consistent with most of my food rules, even though he didn't know them.

There should be a basic health science class that describes how tissues change and the role foods play in making those changes. Everyone who graduates from high school should know how to live in such a way that most diseases cannot gain a foothold in the body. Statistical records show that Americans in the 1990s consumed more food and several hundred more calories per person per day than in the 1950s. We need self-discipline as well as knowledge.

We know enough about food and the laws of nature to avoid obesity as well as nutritional deficiencies. Obesity increases the risk of cancer, heart disease, kidney disease, high blood pressure, diabetes, and other diseases.

If we're going to be effective in taking care of people these days, everyone should recognize that using good nutrition and fresh juices are excellent ways to remain healthy as long as people turn away from lifestyles that undermine health faster than it can be built up. Exercise, fresh air, sunshine, and adequate rest and recreation are important in achieving well-being. But without a foundation of good nutrition, no other therapy can restore health.

Don't expect immediate results from juice therapy. Immediate results are not going to be apparent. Improvement is gradual. This is a gentle art of healing. I tell my patients it takes at least a year before they can get well on the proper foods and juices. So we have to find out where juice therapy fits in our overall diet regimen.

Juicing, taken from a doctor's perspective, would be considered a supplementary therapy to be used with a balanced diet, such as my Health and Harmony Food Regimen. It should not be used by itself unless under a doctor's supervision. A juice diet is dangerous in the hands of an inexperienced person when used for a prolonged period.

My approach to reversal of disease or prevention of disease could be called replacement therapy. We have to replace the old, damaged tissue with healthy, new tissue. We do this by providing the body with a slight excess of all chemical elements in our food regimen to take care of long-standing or short-term deficiencies.

When the constitutionally weak tissues are cleansed and strengthened, the whole body participates in a three- to five-day healing crisis, throwing off old catarrh and toxic encumbrances and building healthy new tissue. This is what natural healing is all about. We don't heal; we take care of chemical deficiencies, and the body heals itself.

This is a wonderful book full of ideas about juicing, blending, and cultivating wellness. Enjoy it, and use it with wisdom.

PART 1

JUICE THERAPY: HOW TO USE JUICES SUCCESSFULLY

CHAPTER 1

HOW JUICE FITS INTO
THE TOTAL DIET PICTURE

I believe juices are the finest means we have of getting all the vitamins, minerals, and enzymes needed (and perhaps just a little extra) to take care of our constitutionally weak organs and tissues, our immune system, and all the vital functions of the body. Juices are wonderful! But, except for an occasional doctor-supervised juice fast, juices must be part of a whole, pure, and natural diet. The human body wasn't meant to thrive on liquids alone, so consider my Health and Harmony Food Regimen below, which was designed to fit the nutritional needs of the great majority of people.

This food regimen, which I developed during years of sanitarium work, is designed to give you principles and guidelines that allow you to take responsibility for the actual food selection. On my health ranch, under my supervision, the cooks chose the foods. But in your house, you will be responsible for choosing the foods. Over the years, I've had the pleasure of seeing many patients grow out of their symptoms just by restoring the chemical balance in their bodies through right nutrition and right living.

DR. JENSEN'S HEALTH AND HARMONY FOOD REGIMEN

Rules of Eating

1. Do not fry foods or use heated oils in cooking. Frying lowers nutritional value, destroys lecithin needed to balance fats, and makes food harder to digest. The temperature at which foods are fried or cooked in oils alters food chemistry, which is not a safe practice. This can be one of the greatest contributing factors to cholesterol formation, hardening of the arteries, and heart disease.

2. Do not eat until you have a keen desire for the plainest food. Too often, we eat simply because it's mealtime, not because we are hungry. Break this undesirable habit. To have the best possible digestion, eat when you are hungry.

3. Do not eat beyond your needs. Overeating is not good for your health.

4. Be sure to thoroughly chew your food. Chewing well increases the efficiency of digestion. You get more food value for the money you spend on food.

5. Miss meals if in pain, emotionally upset, not hungry, chilled, overheated, or ill. Each of these conditions is a signal that we need rest, warmth, calmness, or something other than food, which, if eaten, ties up considerable energy and blood in the gastrointestinal tract. Often, rest is the thing most needed. Food takes energy to digest and involves work by several organs, and it may take hours before food energy is available.

Health and Harmony Food Laws

Food is for building health. You need to have foods that will meet the needs of a vital, active life, and the following laws are designed to do exactly that. These are the kinds of laws that have serious consequences if they are not carried out. If you want to enjoy good health, you have to understand that there are no shortcuts or cheap substitutes. You will have to discipline yourself to follow a "tried-and-true" food regimen like my Health and Harmony Food Regimen.

1. Food should be natural, whole, pure, and fresh. The closer food is to its natural, God-created state, the higher its nutritional value. Some foods, such as meat, potatoes, yams, and grains, must be cooked. Whole foods are more nutritious than refined, bleached, or peeled foods. I'm not telling you to eat banana skins and avocado seeds, I'm just giving you a practical guideline. Pure foods are much better for us than foods with preservatives, artificial colors or flavors, or chemical additives of any kind. Many chemicals now added to commercial food products were never meant to be in the human body. Our bodies were designed for natural, whole, pure, fresh foods, and that's what keeps us in the best condition. We have learned great lessons with experiments on animals using denatured, peeled, and polished foods. They have become sick because the biochemicals needed for good health were left out, and their foods were no longer whole, as God designed them.

2. We should have 60 percent of our foods raw. I am not advising a raw diet because I like the taste, I'm saying it is better for us. Raw foods provide more vitamins, minerals, enzymes, fiber, and bulk because they are "live" foods at the peak of nutritional value if properly selected. Raw foods, such as berries, vegetables, sprouts, nuts, and seeds, help the digestive system and bowel. We have to cook cereal grains, lima beans, artichokes, and other foods, but there are many we can take raw.

3. We should have six vegetables, two fruits, one starch, and one protein every day. Vegetables are high in fiber and minerals. Fruits are high in natural complex sugars and vitamins. Starch is for energy, and protein is for cell repairing and rebuilding, especially of the brain and nerves. This is a balanced combination of foods.

4. Our foods should be 80 percent alkaline and 20 percent acid. We find that 80 percent of the nutrients carried in the blood are alkaline and 20 percent are acid. To keep the blood the way it should be, six vegetables and two fruits make up that 80 percent of alkaline foods we need, while one protein and one starch make up the 20 percent of acid foods. Proteins and many starches are acid-forming, and nearly all the metabolic wastes of the body are acids. We need alkaline-forming foods (fruits and vegetables) so that their alkaline salts will neutralize the acid wastes. I believe we should recognize that to keep the proper alkaline/acid balance in the body we must have six vegetables, two fruits, one starch, and one protein daily. There is no reason why we should add to the acid conditions in our body by consuming too much of the acid-forming foods (proteins and starches). In my experience, acid wastes not properly disposed of are the cause of many disturbances, health problems, and chronic diseases.

5. Vary proteins, starches, vegetables, and fruits from meal to meal and day to day. Every organ of our body needs one chemical element more than others to keep healthy. The thyroid needs iodine, the stomach needs sodium, the blood needs iron, and so on. We also need variety in vitamins. The best way to take care of this is to have variety in foods. Foods, in a way, are matched to our body organs in that many foods are high in one or two minerals and vitamins. But every food is different, and even the same foods grown in different localities and different soils have different arrays of nutrients. As we take in a variety of foods, we must realize that we are made from the dust of the earth. To get calcium foods, we need different kinds of cereal grains, green vegetables, and raw nuts and seeds such as almonds and sesame seeds. Some grains have more calcium than others. To get iron foods, we may go to liver, raisins, and leafy green vegetables. For iodine, we would go to the seafoods. The guiding concept here is variety of foods in the diet to assure that all body tissues are fed the nutrients they need.

6. Eat moderately. The healthiest people I have met in my world travels were the same weight later in life as when they were in their twenties, and some of them were over 120 years of age! In 1998, 55 percent of the people in the United States were overweight according to the National Institutes of Health. This leads to many health problems. Leave that extra food on the plate. Eating at home is more desirable. Many people who eat in restaurants believe they should eat everything on their plate to get their full money's worth. The bigger the waistline, the shorter the lifeline.

7. Separate starches and proteins. Have your proteins and starches at different meals, not because they don't digest well together, but so you will be able to eat more fruits and vegetables each meal. People tend to fill up on protein and starch and neglect their vegetables. I want you to have a lot of vegetables with each meal for your health's sake; when you are hungry, they taste wonderful. There are poor combinations, and I'll mention a few. Dried fruits do not go well with fresh fruits. Unless dried fruits have been reconstituted and brought back to their natural state, it is best not to eat them unless you drink a lot of water along with them. Dried fruits must be reconstituted by putting them in cold water and bringing them to a boil. Let the water boil for about three minutes, then turn off the flame; let it stand overnight. It is best not to have grapefruit and dates together. Melon should always be eaten at least half an hour apart from any other foods. It is best to have your fruit at breakfast and at 3 P.M.

There are a lot of opinions about having liquids with meals. Don't have ice-cold drinks with meals because the cold liquids interfere with digestion. Herb teas and vegetable or fruit juices can be taken with meals since they are foods.

8. Drink at least two quarts of good, *uncontaminated* water every day. That amounts to eight 8-ounce glasses of water daily, not a difficult habit to get into. Most public water systems are highly chemicalized because ground water sources are increasingly polluted. Juices and foods provide a significant amount of water but seldom enough. It is my opinion that high-quality drinking water, either bottled or through reverse osmosis, is a must for good health. Dehydration leads to water imbalance in the body and constipation, processes that increase risk of several diseases. I advise distilled water for those who have arthritis. On hot days, drink more than two quarts of water.

9. Use low-heat, waterless cookware; cook with little or no water; and do not overcook. High heat, boiling in water, and exposure to air are the three greatest robbers of nutrients. Low-heat stainless steel pots with lids that form a water seal are the most efficient means of cooking foods in such a way as to preserve the greatest nutritional value. For oven cooking, glass casserole dishes with lids are fine. I approve of Crock-Pot cooking because it offers another low-heat method. Steamer baskets allow steam cooking at 212 degrees Fahrenheit, and this is acceptable.

10. If you use meat, poultry, and fish, broil or roast it—but have it no more than three times a week. Baking, broiling, and roasting, while far from perfect cooking methods, are at least more acceptable in terms of preserving more nutritional value. Cook at lower heats for longer times to retain the most nutritional value. Avoid fatty meats, and use only white fish with fins and scales. Salmon is permitted, even though it isn't a white meat. Fatty meats lead to obesity, heart trouble, and other health problems. Beef is very stimulating to the heart, and I do not recommend using it. Eating meat more than three times a week can produce excess uric acid and other irritating by-products, causing an unnecessary burden on the body. While I do not believe that the meat itself will cause heart trouble, I believe when we live a fast, hard lifestyle that includes having a large amount of meat, it can lead to heart troubles.

11. Avoid having an excess of one or a few foods in the diet. An excess of one or a few foods may provide too much of certain food chemicals for the body to handle, causing irritation, inflammation, or possible allergies. For example, celiac disease is caused by gluten from wheat and other grains, which damages the wall of the small bowel. Conditions such as diabetes and hypoglycemia are associated with excessive use of sugar. Constipation, catarrh, allergies, and increased risk of heart disease are associated with excessive use of milk products. Arterial and myocardial lesions, which lead to cardiovascular disease and other heart problems, are caused by magnesium deficiency. An excess of one or a few foods also means that other foods are not used in sufficient variety in the diet, which greatly increases the risk of chemical deficiencies.

12. Don't neglect important foods. Our health is determined as much by what we don't eat as well as by what we do eat, leading to nutritional deficiencies that prepare the way for a future disease. If we neglect most vegetables, for example, we prevent our bodies from receiving needed chemical elements and enzymes. Lack of sufficient proteins, carbohydrates, and fats can cause disturbances in the body, as can lack of vitamins, minerals, lecithin, enzymes, and trace elements.

MY HEALTH AND HARMONY FOOD REGIMEN AND THE NEW AMERICAN FOOD PYRAMID

My Health and Harmony Food Regimen was launched decades before the U.S. Food and Drug Administration's "Food Pyramid," with its new health-oriented emphasis on less fats, oils, and sweets but more fruits, vegetables, and cereal products. The FDA is still too meat-and-starch–oriented, in my opinion, but it is going in a healthier direction than in past years. I am glad that my writing, lecturing, and teaching of the past seventy years have played (and still are playing) at least some small part in persuading Americans and the government to be more health-conscious in their food habits and recommendations.

I want to point out that the amounts I have recommended for daily vitamin and mineral intakes in this book were originally developed by the Food and Nutrition Board of the National Research Council, a branch of the National Academy of Sciences. Their old standard term for the amount of each vitamin and mineral we should take daily was *RDA,* which stood for recommended daily allowance. Those RDAs were based on the amounts of food nutrients it would take to keep an "average healthy adult" up and running, so to speak, every day. Since none of us fit the "average" profile, and the great majority of Americans have at least some health problems, the RDAs really don't fit many people. In my opinion, they are too low. But times are changing, and even the government is becoming more interested in our health.

For the past two years, the FDA has been changing the Food and Nutrition Board's RDAs into RDIs (reference daily intakes). RDIs are average values for the entire U.S. population from four-year-old children to adults, and I have used them in this book simply because we have to accept some kind of baseline standard as a working approximation for what each of us actually needs. We can adjust our intake up or down. I encourage you (after you finish reading this book) to find a competent clinical nutritionist or a nutrition-wise doctor to design a vitamin-mineral intake plan that will come up with the right quantities of each nutrient by taking into account your age, sex, weight, work, lifestyle, and home life.

If you can't afford that, you can attempt some do-it-yourself, conservative, trial-and-error adjustments of nutrient amounts to find your best fitness level. Just let your family doctor know what you're doing so that you have a safety net. I have to tell you, I don't believe in meganutrient levels for the simple reason that meganutrients don't occur in nature. I believe the human race evolved from and adapted to a food environment in nature that can't be improved on, except in the sense that we should improve and restore the soil and other natural resources that we have devalued and destroyed in past years. I feel we can and should naturally fine-tune our individual needs with special dietary emphases and food supplements. But we still need some baseline standard to work from.

In chapter 6, you'll encounter the RDIs for all presently known vitamins and minerals essential to human life, so you can intelligently select what you are going to juice. Also in chapter 6, I'll introduce you to the daily reference values (DRVs) that the FDA has designated for more basic nutrient groups, like protein and fats. Using these DRVs, you can take my Health and Harmony Food Laws and transform them into practical meals and snacks of the right kinds and amounts of foods and juices. You can customize my Health and Harmony Food Regimen to fit your needs and your family's needs.

DAILY REFERENCE VALUES FOR BASIC NUTRIENTS FOR EACH FAMILY MEMBER

Nutrient		Quantity
Proteins		50 grams
Carbohydrates		300 grams
Total Fats		65 grams
Saturated fats limit	20 grams	
Unsaturated fats limit	45 grams	
Cholesterol limit	300 milligrams	
Fiber		25 grams
Sodium		2.4 grams
Potassium		3.5 grams

You can adjust the above figures to suit your dietary needs and those of each member of your family. Obviously, you will have to alter the amounts for children and adults, even though the previous chart may have been intended for four-year-olds and up. However, I advise you not to go above the amounts listed for total fats, saturated fats, unsaturated fats, cholesterol, or sodium. Over half the U.S. population is overweight, which is an unnecessary and correctable health risk. If you can reduce the amounts of fats, cholesterol, and table salt sodium you and your family use, go for it. You'll live longer and feel better.

Daily Eating Regimen

Organize your meals to use the food laws and instructions properly. Here is an outline of what your daily food regimen should be like, and this will take care of the food laws—the law of variety, the law of proportions, the law of acid/alkaline balance, the law of 60 percent raw food, and so forth.

You can have half your daily allowance of protein at breakfast and half at dinner; half of your starch at breakfast and half at lunch. Starches and proteins together help keep you from snacking and experiencing hunger between meals, but you shouldn't have so much that you don't have room for vegetables.

Breakfast: ½ starch, ½ protein, health drink
10 A.M.: Vegetable juice or broth
Lunch: 3 vegetables (cooked, raw, or salad), ½ starch, health drink
3 P.M.: Fruit or fruit juice
Dinner: 3 vegetables (cooked, raw, or salad), ½ protein, health drink

Before Breakfast

It is best to have a couple of glasses of water or a drink of some kind before breakfast. This cleanses the bladder and kidneys. I have found the practice of taking a teaspoon of liquid chlorophyll in a glass of water is one of the best things to start the day off. I avoid citrus juices in the morning, as they stir up acids. Remember, citrus stirs up acids, while vegetable juices carry them off. You might include natural, unsweetened fruit juices, such as grape, pineapple, prune, fig, apple, or black cherry.

Breakfast

Eat one fruit, one starch, and a health drink (broth, soup, coffee substitute, buttermilk, raw milk, oat straw tea, alfalfa-mint tea, huckleberry tea, papaya tea, and so on). Dried, unsulfured fruits should be reconstituted. Fresh fruit, such as melon, grapes, apricots, figs, pears, berries, or apple slices (or baked apple), may be sprinkled with ground nuts, seeds, or nut butter. Ground sesame seeds, flaxseeds, sunflower seeds, and almonds are good. Try to use fruit in season. If you have cooked whole grain cereal, sprinkle ground nuts and seeds on top, add chopped dates, raisins, prunes, figs, or other dried fruit for sweetening, or use a little honey or maple syrup. A handful of steamed raisins in any cereal has been a favorite with our family. We can use Swiss muesli any time. Avoid citrus or citrus juices with breakfast, except for an occasional ripe orange, sliced into sections.

Lunch

Have a raw salad with any combination of the following: tomatoes, leaf lettuce (no head lettuce), celery, cucumber, spinach leaves, sprouts (bean, alfalfa, radish, and so on), green pepper, avocado, parsley, watercress, endive, onion, garlic, cabbage, cauliflower, broccoli, and so on. Top with grated carrot, beet, parsnip, or turnip, in any combination. Sprinkle with ground nuts and seeds. Add a little grated cheese, if you like. One or two starches may be used, plus a health drink.

Dinner

Eat one protein, vegetable or fruit salad, one or two cooked vegetables (such as squash, artichoke, cauliflower, spinach, chard, brussels sprouts, broccoli, and so on), and a health drink. If you had a large salad for lunch, have a small one for dinner and vice versa.

Desserts

I do not believe in desserts; however, I occasionally encounter people who believe they have to have it, so here are some suggestions. You can have a sliced apple or raw fruit salad or mixture of cut-up apples and steamed raisins with maple syrup. Another suggestion is to mix plain gelatin with cherry juice and put a little whipped cream on it. Or why not have a banana, apple, pear, apricot, fresh strawberries, or gelatin with fruit?

Suggestions for Preparing Breakfast, Lunch, and Dinner

Breakfast. In many countries, breakfast is considered the main meal because most people believe a good breakfast is necessary to get them going. They believe they have to have something in their bodies to get every organ stimulated and working, and in that stimulated condition, they are ready for work. However, the strength and power to work depends on energy developed in the tissues. The strength we have in the morning comes from our meal at noon the day before. After eating food, it takes some eighteen hours before it gets to the tissues to give strength to our bodies. Once the "response" part of the body—the nervous system—is fed, we have the strength to work. The food we eat at our evening meal will give us our energy tomorrow afternoon. But what we eat for breakfast will be reacting tonight, when we go to bed. This is not the time we should be stimulated. This is one good reason why we should have a light breakfast. We don't want to be ready to go to work at night when it is bedtime. We should have our heavy meal at noon. The strength derived from that comes just in time to start our day right the following morning.

Preparing whole grain cereals. The best way is to use a wide-mouthed thermos. Put the cereal grain into the bottle, cover with boiling water, and let it soak overnight. Make sure there's room for the cereal to expand without breaking the thermos. *Exception:* Cornmeal must always be added to cold water in a pan and brought to a boil or it lumps. When it has boiled, pour the mixture into a thermos and leave it overnight. Cereal can also be cooked in a double boiler.

Ground nuts and seeds. You can add psyllium husks, wheat bran, wheat germ, oat bran, flaxseed meal, ground nuts and seeds, dulse, or vegetable broth powder seasoning on many foods to add fiber, flavor, and nutritional value. Herbs are a fine addition.

The main thing we are trying to establish in our diet work is what is right for a person and not who is right. There must be some regular or definite program that fits most people. The word *breakfast* comes from the original "break fast." Whenever we fast or go without food all night long, digestive juices flow slower. Our whole body is working slower. Therefore, when we awaken, we should break the fast with fruit juice or a light nourishing drink of some other kind. Then we should have a fruit breakfast. Fruit is the proper thing to break a fast. If we like, a little protein is a good combination with fruit, and it may be allowed. We can also have restored dried fruits and carbohydrates together for breakfast. The idea of having fried foods, a lot of muffins, bread or French toast, and other heavy foods is not right. It is not a matter of seeing how much we can eat.

Lunch. If you want energy for the next morning, eat a good lunch. That "washed-out" feeling with which so many people start the day is probably due to the fact they can't always be bothered to fix a nourishing meal for themselves at midday. They may eat a sandwich with white bread and a filling with no nutritional value and a cup of coffee.

We follow along with the starch idea at noon only because most people are in the habit of having sandwiches or bread for this meal. Make sure your sandwiches are made of thinly sliced, whole grain breads stuffed heartily with good fillings and plenty of vegetables to aid the digestion. Avocado, grated carrot, celery, and nuts; cottage cheese and alfalfa sprouts; olives and lettuce; nuts and dates; and sunflower seed meal with honey are a few suggestions. Use a spoonful of health mayonnaise, cream cheese, or mashed banana to stick them together. Flavor with vegetable seasonings and dulse. Along with your sandwiches, eat extra salad ingredients such as green leaves, carrot and celery sticks, green peppers, cucumbers, or tomatoes. A health cookie is permissible, but wouldn't a bag of nuts, sunflower or squash seeds, raisins, dates, or figs be more pleasing?

Did you know you can make sandwiches without bread? Bread is not the only starch; in fact, it is one of the least desirable, and even if you pack a lunch, other starches are just as convenient. Slice an apple horizontally and wedge cheese between the slices, for instance. Raw baby zucchini slices make a nice "bread" to stuff with nut butter; some people use raw, thinly sliced eggplant filled with a tasty mayonnaise spread. Even lettuce leaves will enclose many tasty, nourishing fillings.

Starches. Yellow cornmeal, baked potato, ripe or baked banana, yam, sweet potato, barley, rye, millet, brown rice, wild rice (actually this is a seed), buckwheat, and squash, such as banana, acorn, or spaghetti, are all starches. A couple of dead-ripe bananas can become the hub of your lunch.

Never forget variety. Use a thermos to hold your cold fruit or vegetable cocktail in summer, your hot broth or herb tea in winter. It can also hold a cool fruit whip or soy, rice, or nut milk beverages.

Lunchtime is salad time. You will be on the move again shortly, and it takes exercise to process raw food. Have your big, green, raw salad at noon, using as many vegetables as possible. It is amazing the number we can use raw, such as summer squash, asparagus, Jerusalem artichokes, okra, cauliflower, and turnips, to mention just a few. These can be extremely tasty grated and occasionally dressed with a tangy mayonnaise. For visual appeal, sometimes stuff a green pepper, tomato, or celery stalks. (These can even be carried to work in a jar. So can salads, although they lose value if left cut up too long. It is best to take vegetables along whole.)

Have a cooked, low-starch vegetable with your meal, too, if you like. When serving a root vegetable, always make sure you have a "top" vegetable, whose edible part is above ground, with it but not necessarily the matching top or green. For example, if you have beets, don't serve the greens with it. Instead, you might serve beets with steamed spinach. On colder days, a nourishing soup is welcome. And why not try a cool, raw soup in summer?

Finish your meal with a health drink such as herb tea, dandelion coffee, buttermilk, raw milk, whey, or any good health beverage.

It really doesn't take very long to prepare a lunch such as what we suggested, and the lift it will give your vitality and good humor will be well worth it.

Dinner. If you value your health, eat often at home! No one suffers more from malnutrition than the clergyman and his wife, who are often asked out to supper, who attend church luncheons, or who go out to men's or women's prayer breakfasts.

Dinner should be a family affair, a happy get-together at the end of the day when news can be exchanged convivially at the family dinner table. Here, children can learn by example the rules of healthy eating, a happy attitude, quiet enjoyment, manners, cultivation of a desire for plain food, eating slowly and masticating, and most important, knowing when to stop eating.

Use the evening meal to balance your day nutritionally. If you skimped on your salad at noon, have a bigger one at dinner or begin the meal with a raw vegetable cocktail. Did you get your quota of two fruits today? Have a fruit dessert or Waldorf salad for dinner. A mixed vegetable broth is an excellent way to bring up your vegetable intake for the day—there are very good recipes for raw soups, too.

Plan your dinner around this basic formula: a small raw salad, two cooked vegetables, one protein, and a health drink. If you are not a vegetarian, have meat two or three times a week, but make sure it is lean meat and cooked by broiling or roasting without fat. Fish once a week is a good protein high in iodine and phosphorus. Choose fish with fins and scales and steam, grill, or bake it. Two nights a week serve a cheese dish. You'll find a popular summer supper is plain cheeses with fruit. Cheese that breaks easily, such as Roquefort, feta, or gorgonzola, or cottage cheese and a variety of fruits make a complete meal. An egg dish, such as a soufflé, omelet, or poached or scrambled eggs on spinach or other greens, can complete the week's dinners.

Nuts are among our recommended protein sources, and among them the almond is king. Nuts are best eaten raw. Always soak nuts for several hours in fruit juice, tea, or honey water for better digestion. Nut butter is good for snacks or meals. Beans, lentils, split peas, and sunflower seeds can also be used. An excellent vegetarian protein made from soybeans is tofu or soy cheese. The soy substitute meats are always permissible.

With your protein dish, take a small raw salad. Vary this from day to day. It is good to have a sulfur vegetable (cabbage or onion family) along with proteins. The two cooked vegetables can be of any of the nonstarchy type. Remember the value of greens and eat plenty of them.

Your beverage may be a broth or soup. Vary beverages with all the different herb teas, whey, raw milk, or buttermilk.

It is permissible to have a health dessert at this protein meal, although the idea is not highly recommended. Fresh, raw fruit is best.

You may exchange your noon meal for the evening meal, but follow the same regimen. This is sometimes a good idea, especially if you have trouble getting to sleep. Starches predispose one to sleep more than proteins, which are more stimulating.

No matter how wonderful the dinner, remember that if you are emotionally upset, chilled, overheated, ill, or lacking the keenest desire for plain food, miss the meal! That will do you more good than eating. Have a glass of freshly prepared juice instead.

When you plant good seed in well-mineralized soil, the result is healthy, hardy plants, free of disease and resistant to insects. In the same way, when you put a wholesome balance of foods and fresh juices into bodies with good digestion and assimilation, you get people free of disease and resistant to the various disturbances that come to the average person who lacks a balanced diet. Fresh juices are essential in any balanced food regimen.

Juices feed the tissues, energize the body, help prevent disease, and add vitality and sparkle to wellness! Now that you know the "whys" and "wherefores," do yourself a favor and make juicing and juices a natural and regular part of your lifestyle! You'll be glad you did!

Rules for Getting Well—It's Up to You to Keep These Rules

1. Learn to accept whatever decision is made. Do your best to keep your peace of mind. Peace is a healer.

2. Let the other person make a mistake and learn. This is so much better than standing over people and supervising every move. Learn to give the person the opportunity to grow and grow up. We are bound to make mistakes. Let's not gloat over them or live in remorse about them.

3. Learn to forgive and forget. Many studies have now shown that forgiving enhances health and helps prevent chemical changes in the body that may lead to disease.

4. Be thankful and bless people. These are two of the main secrets to a healthy life.

5. Live in harmony—even if it is good for you.

6. Don't talk about your misfortunes or illnesses. It doesn't do any good for you or the person you tell, and it prevents an opportunity for them to do the same to you. Save it for your doctor. He or she is paid to listen to your troubles.

7. Don't gossip. Gossip that comes through the grapevine is usually sour grapes.

8. Spend ten minutes a day meditating on how you can become a better person. Replace negative thoughts with positive ones.

9. Exercise daily. Keep your spine and joints limber, develop your abdominal muscles, and expand your lungs with specific exercises on a regular schedule.

10. Walk ten minutes barefoot in the dewy grass or sand the first thing in the morning to stimulate the blood circulation.

11. Do not smoke or drink alcohol. Both nicotine and alcohol are depressant drugs. Both require energy to detoxify the body, energy needed for more useful life processes.

12. Go to bed by 9 P.M., at the latest, when you can. If you are tired during the day, rest. Rest allows the body to give its full attention and energy to healing and rebuilding tissues. Write down your problems at the end of the day and forget them. Get a good night's sleep. Then, go over them first thing in the morning when you are refreshed, so that you can look at them with a fresh mind and body.

CHAPTER 2

THE DOCTOR VIEWS
JUICE THERAPY

I don't remember when it first dawned on me that a fresh, delightful glass of juice with breakfast was much more than just a nice way to start the day. But, by the time I began to operate my first "live-in" health ranch, I knew that juices—both fruit and vegetable—were good for therapy. They could even save lives.

For one thing, I had a few patients who couldn't take anything but liquids. Their digestive systems, for one reason or another, were not tolerating solid foods well. So I was feeding them broths, carrot juice, herbal teas, and warm, foamy goat's milk, straight from the doe. (I had goats in those days to make fresh milk available to my patients. I still keep a few for my own good.) I watched my patients gain strength until they were up and walking around. When they were up to taking solid foods again, I still gave them juices as a regular part of their therapy. It is extremely important for anyone in a delicate level of health, whether they are getting better or worse at a particular time, to have slightly more than enough nutritional support.

Many diseases are favored or even "invited," in some sense, when nutrient deficiencies have preceded them. Many diseases are accompanied by nutrient deficiencies as they develop; others create nutrient deficiencies by their effects on body chemistry and tissue integrity. A few diseases are caused and sustained only by nutritional deficiencies (pellagra, scurvy, osteoporosis, and so on). Juice supplements function as effective therapy in all these cases.

The most important lesson a person can learn is that nature will heal if we let her. She can do it, but she needs the opportunity.

Our food intake quality is very important. It's time we recognize that inadequate food intake is "on the other end" of every symptom in the body. There is no disease that isn't accompanied by a chemical shortage due to increased use (and eventual depletion) of vitamins and minerals by stressed body systems, and it is time we realize that if these chemical shortages are taken care of, we wouldn't be treating a disease. Juicing helps build the whole body by providing a rich supply of chemical elements.

Adults weighing 150 pounds have about 3 to 4 pounds of calcium in their bodies and need 1,000 milligrams of calcium per day (sometimes more). According to the National Institutes of Health (NIH), a large percentage of Americans do not get enough calcium. In fact, the average adult woman gets only about 635 milligrams of calcium daily. In members of both sexes who are sixty-five years of age or older, daily calcium intake of less than 600 milligrams is common. Calcium deficiency has recently been linked to premenstrual syndrome by researchers from St. Luke's-Roosevelt Hospital Center in New York. We find that osteoporosis and osteomalecia are the best-known calcium-deficiency diseases, but there are others. Oral bone loss, colon cancer, hypertension, and preeclampsia, a pregnancy disorder, are believed to be affected by calcium deficiency.

The best natural sources of calcium include milk and milk products, nuts, green vegetables, beans, and broccoli. There are many people who do not tolerate milk products well, so the following chart shows other sources of calcium and the amounts needed.

FOOD SOURCES OF CALCIUM			
Cheese (1½ ounces)	306 mg	Cooked broccoli (1 cup)	178 mg
Milk (8 ounces)	300 mg	Vegetarian baked beans (1 cup)	127 mg
Almonds (½ cup)	189 mg	Cooked kale (1 cup)	94 mg

The NIH recommends 1,500 milligrams of calcium for men and women over sixty-five. As you can see, those who choose not to use dairy products will have a difficult time getting the calcium they need through foods. One of the best calcium supplements is calcium citrate, which doesn't interfere with iron assimilation. Postmenopausal women are also encouraged to take estrogen, which reduces loss of bone calcium. Optimum intake of any vitamin or mineral usually involves taking several nutrients together. In the case of calcium, phosphorus, magnesium, manganese, copper, zinc, and vitamins A, C, and D are necessary for proper assimilation.

DON'T BE MISLED: THE TRUTH IS GOOD ENOUGH FOR ALL OF US

Let us get off the ideas now that juices are going to cure diabetes, that juices are going to cure cancer, that juices are going to cure anything! What we are going to do is work in harmony with nature, and nature will do the curing. Yes, I use juices as part of my program. Nature created our bodies to be self-building, self-repairing, and self-rejuvenating. This happens automatically when you're sleeping, working, or attending classes, without any conscious effort on your part. However, when we are working too hard at the office, we break down our bodies through mental exhaustion. The nervous system comes out short if you don't have the proper balance in your lifestyle. Juices help.

We can become chemically deficient in any of the different systems in our body. A nutrient deficiency may affect the various functions in the respiratory system, the urinary system, the glandular system, or the nervous system. What do you suppose will happen if we do not have some of the nutrients to replace those used up during the day? What happens when we use up the body's available chemical resources? We become chemically short, the affected body tissues malfunction, and the resulting symptoms may be treated as a disease. I want you to know that every disease is a definite sign of chemical shortages somewhere in the body. Nature cures, but she must have the right chemical elements to work with. The juices that nature provides can prevent or reverse the chemical shortages that give disease a foothold in the body.

The Bircher-Benner Institute in Zurich, Switzerland, a pioneering health spa built in 1897, was trying to help their most hopeless cases with juices and vegetarian diets. I saw such wonderful recoveries in some of their patients that I could hardly believe my eyes. I wondered if I could duplicate their success with my own patients.

I am not the only doctor who realizes this, but I'll tell you, in the early years of my sanitarium practice, it was a revelation to me to find out that a balanced diet of whole, pure, natural, and mostly fresh foods could bring patients with advanced chronic diseases back to health—not all of them, of course, but most of them. Juices were always part of their food regimen.

Although not all my patients were fully restored to health, I found that all patients, whatever their problems, responded to improved diet. I have many case histories where diabetic people improved, lessening their use of insulin. I have seen open, running leg ulcers healed—in one case by using green vegetable juices alone, in other cases by a combination of improved diet and bowel cleansing.

FOODS ARE NOT MEDICINES

I am totally committed to treating people through proper nutrition, but the first thing I want you to realize is that the foods are not doing the curing, they're only assuring that you have all that nature needs in order to make a good body. Foods do not heal. Foods provide the resources for the body to heal itself. This is done automatically when the right nutrients are available. When they aren't available, drugs alone can't do a complete job of tissue restoration. Neither can any other therapy. In cases of imbalanced, incomplete, nutrient-deficient diets, diseases—from the acute to the chronic—linger on. We must have the chemical material to restore function at the cell level to its natural, normal state. Complete, balanced nutrition makes it possible for us to be vigorous and strong enough to do our jobs, to have good marriages, and to take care of all the challenges that come along in life.

I consider regular use of fresh fruit and vegetable juices to be one of the very best ways of making sure we have the fitness and good health to live and work at our very best. I have been working with clinical nutrition now for many years and have seen many wonderful results, but I don't have the laboratory evidence to prove that complete tissue restoration, complete healing, takes place. However, I believe it does. There's hardly a case that comes in that I don't have some medical laboratory tests showing significant improvements when patients are fed properly, even after years of long-term deficiencies.

Doctors Make a Living on Your Living

It is in this neglect of nutrition where doctors make their living. It is due to this neglect that we find all kinds of symptoms— sixteen thousand symptoms and symptom combinations have been recorded for the different ailments, disturbances, and diseases including insomnia, shortness of breath, heart arrhythmia, diverticula, skin rashes, bowel toxemia, and so on. You can go right down the line, and every single one of these symptoms can be helped with nutritional means, especially through the use of fresh fruit and vegetable juices.

Perhaps it isn't as important to have complete laboratory confirmation of healing than a visible improvement in the person's body, a new sense of well-being, and an increased energy level. Is the patient feeling better? Does he still need medication? Is her level of physical activity back up to what it used to be? Is the patient pleased with his or her quality of life? We shouldn't be satisfied with only symptom relief, where you and your doctor are just coddling the disease and the symptoms. That invites disaster down the line. In dealing with a health problem, our objective should always be to find the root of the problem and do everything we can to deal with it and bring the patient to wholeness.

We know that our greatest reservoir of wisdom is in the elderly people in our nation. Yet, we do not take care of the elderly properly. Nor will they have good health at the end of their lives if they are not taking good care of themselves at a younger age. What you do today and tomorrow can have harsh consequences ten or twenty years from now, or why would the American Cancer Society tell us it takes twenty years to build some types of cancer? Where was the doctor in the beginning? Are people using any preventive means? It's a temporary occupation that we have in this physical body, and it's going to be very temporary if we don't use the right nutritional support. The older we grow, the more valuable juices become, because they are easily digested and assimilated.

Do you believe it's time to replenish that body of yours with vitamins, minerals, and other nutrients? I'll tell you about one of the greatest ways I know to do it.

Vegetable and Fruit Juice Therapy

Regarding vegetable and fruit juice therapy, it's not a matter of curing a disease. I want to make sure you have the proper understanding of what is going on. What we are doing with vegetable and fruit juice therapy is to transfer vitamins and vital minerals—as contained in juices—into the body and its fluids (blood and lymph). This initiates a gradual cleansing process. First, the lymph stream cannot be clean unless we have the proper minerals available to the lymph system. If lymph is overloaded with toxic material, if it is polluted with chemical toxins from bad air, bad water, food additives, and poison sprays that have been used on foods, we cannot expect the lymph system to be capable of doing its job of cleansing the body and protecting it against bacteria and viruses.

The best cleansing that I can possibly think of is by using the vitamin-rich, mineral-rich vegetable and fruit juices. If we could put pure water into our bodies that was rich in bio-organic calcium (not the calcium compounds found in heavily mineralized spring waters), we would eventually start a cleansing process.

JUICES ARE MOSTLY FOR CLEANSING

We need to have balanced amounts of cleansing and building in the body. It should be a fifty/fifty proposition. If you're going to go through a process involving 75 percent elimination and 25 percent building program, you're on an imbalanced diet. Junk foods constitute a diet just as living on grape juice or carrot juice entirely must be considered a diet. Living entirely on juice is a diet. We have to eventually get back to a healthy way of living. My Health and Harmony Food Regimen, presented in chapter 1, is the goal we must always work toward. A truly balanced diet is always half cleansing (removing undesirable toxins and catarrh from the tissues) and half building (repairing and restoring tissue integrity).

People often underestimate the potency and effectiveness of juices. In the 1930s, Dr. H. E. Kirschner of Olive View Sanitarium in Los Angeles came to see me about a patient of mine who had cured himself of a terminal disease by living only on carrot juice for over a year. Dr. Kirschner was a medical doctor who believed in the healing power of foods. He had talked to my patient, Del Wilhite of Azusa, California, and was convinced of the truthfulness of his story, and he came to me for my side of it.

I told him, "Del came to me after his doctors had given up on him. He had been diagnosed as having cancer of the bowel and could hardly eat anything. I put him on carrot juice, because nearly anyone can take it, and it agreed well with him. He lost a good deal of weight for a while, but his weight stabilized. In addition to the carrot juice, he took liquid chlorophyll occasionally. He passed some unusual material from his bowel during the course of his juice fast. At the end of the year, he went back to the hospital for a checkup. *His hospital report proved that he was absolutely free of the cancer!* This was a very wonderful thing for him, and, of course, he was overjoyed. He was able to go back to a regimen of solid foods, but he was careful to use whole, pure, and natural foods to make sure he kept his healing."

Dr. Kirschner was so impressed with this case that he wrote an article about it and sent it to a medical journal to show what juices could do for a person. The article was returned to him along with a note saying the story lacked credibility and that it wasn't up to the medical profession to promote any particular food for the healing of any disease. Dr. Kirschner said, "I have visited this man and I can hardly believe the good health he is in. I believe his story."

Dr. Kirschner developed his own organic garden in Yucaipa, California, where his employees raised vegetables and herbs for his patients. He believed in natural healing through foods and juices and wrote several books about his successes with patients. I'll have more to say about him later in this book.

More recently, beta-carotene (which is abundant in carrots) has been tested on laboratory rats and mice and has been shown to prevent or reverse certain types of cancers induced in these laboratory animals. Research into the anticarcinogenic properties of beta-carotene (provitamin A) is continuing.

THE PLACE FOR JUICES

The function that juices provide best is to help balance a diet that emphasizes more building than it should. Such a diet typically overstresses proteins and starches with not enough fruits and vegetables, which are needed for their vitamins, minerals, fiber, and ability to stimulate the elimination channels. To repair or replace any damaged cells in the body, it is necessary that our juices contain the chemical elements required to build new molecular structures. This takes fluids that transmit the vital energies of the sun, air, and water so they can reach every cell in the body.

Cells in the body have a very close connection with the blood through the interstitial fluid that surrounds cells. The cells are only as clean as the blood that releases both nutrients and toxins (if any) into the interstitial fluid. If you are going to live a healthy life, you must keep the blood as clean as possible and as nutrient-rich as possible. Emphasizing juices will promote cellular respiration and energy production for cleansing. Some people can go on indefinitely on an elimination-promoting juice diet, while others cannot. Use good sense. Usually, I regard juices as a supplement to a regular, balanced diet, but there are conditions that can only be helped with juices in a radical elimination program. I advise you to do this only under the supervision of a doctor.

SPECIAL DIETING PROCEDURES

Special diets may be tailored to restore chemical balance to the body structures you may have weakened in the last twenty years or so by wrong food and lifestyle habits. It's not always what you eat that counts, it's what you digest and assimilate. You must chew your food adequately. You must take care of your gastrointestinal system. You must exercise enough to force the circulating blood to visit and feed every cell in the body.

Juicing forces out the vital nutrients held within the fruit or vegetable fibers. Is it possible that trace elements in those juices are needed in various parts of your body? Why is it that the trace minerals selenium, boron, and zinc are selling so well in the health food stores when you could get them in freshly juiced vegetable or fruit juices?

Juices will help compensate for what you may not have been eating for years. The problem isn't always what you eat. Many times, it's what you didn't eat. You starved your body of certain nutrients. Did you get enough zinc? Zinc promotes enzyme activity and supports the immune system. Did you get enough selenium? Selenium protects against cancer. How about boron? Boron assists in calcium assimilation and is especially needed by the elderly. When boron isn't in the soil, for example, the leaves of avocado trees turn brown and begin to drop off. Farmers call this a disease, and we begin to see many symptoms of plant diseases come on when the soil lacks certain minerals needed to produce healthy crop growth.

THE ABUNDANCE OF NUTRIENTS IN JUICES

Fruit and vegetables grown in mineral-rich soil are loaded with vitamins, minerals, enzymes, bioflavonoids, phytochemicals, and carotenoids. We find that nutrients soluble in juices are easiest to digest and assimilate in the body. When we are sick, many vitamins, such as the B-complex vitamins and vitamin C, and minerals, such as zinc, copper, selenium, and iron, are used up faster than usual. That's why sick people have no vitality, no energy, no get-up-and-go. Nor do sick people digest or assimilate foods well. A tired, fatigued body does not get much value from solid foods taken in.

This is the time to use juices. When we are sick and fatigued, the effect of juices seems like a touch of the miraculous. Energy and alertness are restored. We sleep better. The immune system is being supported and is attacking any microorganisms that don't belong in the body. Tissues, glands, and organs are being protected. There are twenty active vitamins needed by your body and seventeen minerals and trace elements. You can get them all in juices.

PREPARE YOUR FOOD FOR EASY DIGESTION

Vegetable juices, fruit juices, and liquefied foods are more easily digested than solid foods (whether raw or cooked). It is not what you eat that counts, but what you digest and absorb. If you don't absorb the mineral elements from your foods, you're going to end up with chemical deficiencies.

I have often mentioned how effectively our natural food program has been over the years in my health ranch work, where over one hundred thousand patients have been blessed by a food regimen that emphasized juices and herbal teas. We needed 3,000 pounds of carrots a month, and lesser amounts of other vegetables and fruits, just to make juices available every morning at 10 o'clock for our patients. To make sure the vegetables and fruits were grown organically in the very best soil, we grew our own vegetables. Since we cared for our patients, we served vegetable and fruit juices to them. If you want to make sure your body gets the very best, use organic juices. The life you save may be your own.

A STATEMENT BY ONE OF OUR GREAT MEDICAL DOCTORS, TOM SPIES, M.D.

Tom Spies, M.D., was honored by the American Medical Association in 1957 for his great contribution to the healing art through his work with foods. Here is how he summed up his observations:

> All diseases are caused by chemicals. All diseases can be cured by chemicals. All the chemicals used by the body except for the oxygen, which we breathe, and the water, which we drink, are taken in through food. If we only knew enough, all diseases could be prevented and could be cured through proper nutrition.
>
> As tissues become damaged, they lack the chemicals for good nutrition. They tend to become old. They lack what I call 'tissue integrity.' There are people of forty whose brains and arteries are senile. If we could help the tissues repair themselves by correcting nutritional deficiencies, we can make old age wait.

How did he ever come to these conclusions? There's hope and inspiration in this doctor who opened his eyes and took a different viewpoint. The wise person is always willing to consider the value of an alternative view.

IT HURTS TO BE ON THE CUTTING EDGE

How do you suppose I felt when newspaper articles in the 1990s began to announce the "discovery" of new facts about foods that I'd been using and teaching my patients forty years ago? One article said they have now found that vegetables are good for preventing cancer. Another announced that less insulin is needed by diabetics when they use the proper foods. A third piece told how birth defects in children could be avoided if mothers used a balanced diet during pregnancy. But they missed something important. What a great thing it would be if we were willing to assure ourselves of having healthy children by looking carefully after our own health twenty years before they are conceived.

LET'S LOOK AT THE "LIFE FACTOR"

In 1923, seeds were found in King Tut's newly discovered tomb. They were over three thousand years old. The first of these ancient Egyptian peas was planted on January 19, 1945, and later eaten. It proved to have a very appetizing flavor. It's this "life factor" in the foods we need. We have to have live foods.

It is also the "life factor" that makes juices such a wonderfully valuable supplement to a balanced diet. To get this vital material into your body, the fruits and vegetables we juice have to be alive. In some of the two-hundred-year-old monasteries in Florida, they found flower seeds and planted them, and they grew. Why? Nature is interested in the next generation. She's so interested, she produces a protective hull around seeds. Similarly, there is a protective membrane around fruit or vegetable cell complexes containing juices. The protective membrane protects the group of nutrients that I associate with the "life factor."

Some vegetables, nuts, and seeds contain the high-powered principles and chemical activities that are needed to renew glands, such as the pituitary, thyroid, adrenals, prostate, ovaries, testes, and so on. When we take in the "gland-building factors," we help the whole body. This is not taking care of the disease, this is taking care of the chemical deficiencies. And this is what vegetable juices and liquefied foods should be used for. This is another reason we should use live foods.

LIVE FOODS

Mae West was once my patient and followed many of my suggestions in her dieting program. One of her famous lines was, "You know, I'm not interested in the men in my life, I'm interested in the life in my men." With this thought in mind, I think we should be interested in the life in our foods. The life in our fruits and vegetables is so powerfully influenced by the sunshine that many times juice is called "liquid sunshine." Indirectly, our lives are enhanced by the soil that feeds the plants we eat and the water that carries the life-giving nutrients throughout each plant. We need to take good care of our soil and clean up our water sources.

Soluble mineral elements separate into positively and negatively charged ions in solution. They create micro-sized electrical fields, and I believe these are properties that assist in healing. I believe people cannot be well without them. This is the most important information you'll ever get in your life. If you want to reach out for the greatest possible health, clean up your lifestyle, juice a variety of the "live" foods, and drink a glass three times daily. You must do this in the context of a balanced food regimen.

WHAT YOU NEED TO KNOW TO GET STARTED

You will need a good juicer and a good blender. I will discuss these in some detail in chapter 3, but you must read the operating instructions and you must take good care of your equipment to get the most out of them. Avoid the cheaper machines, and check out what's available before you buy. Know what you want to do with your equipment: If you only want to juice hard vegetables like carrots, celery, and beets, a centrifugal juicer will be all you need. If you want to juice apples or citrus, you'll have to get something else. If you know you want to juice wheat grass or spinach, you will have to get a special juicer that handles leafy vegetation.

It is very important to understand that freshly made juices have the highest nutritional value, and fresh, organically grown fruits and vegetables at peak ripeness (fruits and some vegetables) or not quite mature (young vegetables) have the highest concentration of nutrients. Use fruits and vegetables at the peak of nutritional value, juice them right away, and drink the juice right away. That's the idea. If you pick a raspberry at its full, soft ripeness right off the vine and pop it into your mouth, that's the most nutritional ripeness you'll get out of it. Get it?

Oxidation, aging, spoiling, heating, and soaking in water are processes that dilute or destroy vitamins, minerals, and trace elements and render fruits or vegetables less nutritious for juicing.

Plan your juicing strategy: (1) when and where you will get your foods for juicing; (2) when you will actually juice them; and (3) when you will be drinking the juice. Always cover and refrigerate any juice you intend to save for later.

PEAK NUTRITION IS IN PEAK RIPENESS

When you see a ripe berry, pick it and eat it or juice it (and others nearby). Don't save it for a week. It'll never do you any good after keeping it that long. Don't bother to pick a berry when it is green. You know it will taste sour, but also it doesn't have the nutritional value of a ripe fruit. You must juice it right on the button, when it's ripe. That's why they say in Boston they've never tasted a ripe blackberry. Why? Because they don't get ripe berries in Boston; they are shipped green from other parts of the country.

When string beans are picked off the vine, they're alkaline-forming. In six days of storage, they become acid-forming. You can see by this example why you should juice fruit or vegetables soon after picking. For the same reason—loss of nutritional value—it's important to drink juice right after making it. We should get it to the digestive juices before any oxidation has taken place.

Healing begins when the right minerals and vitamins reach the tissue in need of nutritional support. And if you can see that healing continues through perseverance, having this day in and day out, you'll finally remold, revitalize, remake, and refresh the body tissues damaged by disease and nutritional deficiencies. This is how we restore the integrity that we need in the makeup of every compromised cell in our body.

Remember, we reach every cell in our body through the blood and through interstitial fluid derived from the blood, and, by means of the blood, soluble biochemical nutrients reach every cell in the body. That's why it is so important to make and drink fresh juices and juice combinations three or more times per day.

Juices play a wonderful, healing role in my life, promoting healthy, fully nourished tissues, glands, organs, and systems; in essence, wellness at its best. Let us get away from the idea of trying to cure a disease. Let us make a healthy body, chemically complete, fit for tomorrow and ready to meet any of the challenges of our lives.

CHAPTER 3

STARTING OUT WITH JUICES

Fresh fruit and vegetable juices can often add such a valuable nutritional boost to our regular diet that we notice a wonderful difference in how we feel after only a month or two. In a year's time of regular daily use of a variety of fresh juices, who knows what can happen? Relief from long-standing chronic disease is the reward of many who decide to change to a healthy diet and lifestyle—and stick with it!

I believe juices should be a regular part of everyone's daily food regimen. And, with the availability of wonderful, moderately priced juicers, anyone can become an expert in juicing.

In days gone by, Grandpa and Grandma drank apple juice made fresh from big, manually operated apple presses. Grandma, if she lived in a region where citrus wasn't too expensive, made hand-squeezed orange juice by pushing cut orange halves back and forth over a small fluted dome in the middle of a shallow dish that caught and held the juice and pulp until there was enough to pour in a glass. Sometimes grape juice was made by mashing grapes in a colander and collecting the juice in a bowl below it, then putting the grape pulp in a clean flour sack to drip into the juice bowl until the last drop was gathered. In those days, I believe juice was more highly regarded than it is now because it was harder to come by and required more work. But now that we know how much benefit we derive from juices, we should be eager to take advantage of the opportunity to live healthier, more energetic lives by making fresh juices a regular part of our lifestyle.

A NOTE OF CAUTION

On one hand, I'm pleased to see so many different juices and juice combinations and juice cocktails on the supermarket shelves—not to mention all the frozen juices ready to thaw, dilute, and make up as soon as you get home. *But these are not fresh juices, and they don't have the nutritional value of fresh juices.* If it was made last week or last year, what's fresh about it?

I'm suggesting that you beware of juices in bottles, cans, or cartons. Such juices may be made either from fruit concentrates or imported fruits from countries that still use pesticides banned in the United States, such as DDT and others known to increase cancer risk. Or they may be grown on soil depleted of important nutrients, which means that the fruit juice will lack nutrients. Juice cocktails may contain added sugar. I'm not saying that all bottled, canned, or cartoned juices are contaminated or terribly inferior. I'm saying they are seldom, if ever, as tasty or nutritionally potent as fresh juices. And they may contain artificial chemical additives. Many times juices are diluted with water.

What's wrong with chemical food or commercial drink additives? Basically, they are not natural to the body and they have to be detoxified, broken down, and eliminated from the body just like any other foreign substance taken in. This robs the body of energy, ties up an unknown portion of immune system defenses, and may contribute to liver damage. If there ever was such a thing as a "harmless" food additive, it could still become a carcinogen or poison by combining with another chemical or drug residue present in the system. I don't know about you, but I'd rather not take the chance. I prefer my foods—including juices—to be whole, pure, natural, and fresh!

SIMPLY STARTING AND STARTING SIMPLY

It doesn't take much to get started in juicing single fruits or vegetables. You just buy a juicer and get going.

Shop around and find out what kinds of juicers are available. You'll find there are still hand-operated juicers that work well with citrus fruits but not much else. I don't advise buying one because I believe most people use too much citrus and use too little of the many other juices available. So, live a little and sample some of the wonderful variety of juices from the many fruits in God's garden.

Look into electric juicers and find one in your price range that fits your needs. You might want to check in the consumer magazines in your local library to see what they have to say about the comparative merits of the different juicers, and which ones are the best buys for the money.

You also need to learn how to pick out good fruits and vegetables for juicing, which I address in chapter 5. You should know that unsprayed, organically raised fruits and vegetables, grown on naturally fertilized, full mineralized soil (including all the trace elements we need) are the best buys and superior, nutritionally, to any juices sold in stores.

After you've made some of the "single fruit" juices, you'll be ready to think about combining flavors and nutrients by mixing juices, or by adding other supplements to them in a blender.

JUICERS AND BLENDERS: A BIG DIFFERENCE

Juicers and blenders are made to do very different tasks. Most juicers have only one speed, while blenders have many speeds, but that's not the essential difference. The main difference is that juicers grind fruits and vegetables to pulp, then extract the juice from the pulp for you. Blenders either liquefy what is put in them or cut it into fine pieces. In other words, the pulp and juice are mixed together in one somewhat mushy mass.

Of course, you can extract juice with your juicer and combine the juice with other ingredients in a blender, to make some delicious and very nourishing combinations. For example, you can juice equal amounts of carrots and celery to make a lovely combination. Pour this juice into a blender (about a pint, for example), then add one-fourth cup of raw sunflower seeds that you've soaked overnight in pineapple juice, and blend until the seeds are well liquefied. The taste will surprise and please you, and this combination is rich in vitamin E, fatty acids, zinc, and many wonderful enzymes. It's a great health builder for the glands.

If you don't have a blender, I encourage you to get one. If you can only get one new appliance at this time, however, buy the juicer first and the blender later. Part 2 of this book, "Blending Naturally for Health and Wellness," will be of interest to those who prefer blending.

SOME FACTS OF LIFE ABOUT JUICERS

You can get a good centrifugal juicer, such as the Acme or Omega, that will juice "hard vegetables" like carrots, celery, beets, and so forth, by grinding them up on a spinning grinder plate, then throwing the pulp against the side of a spinning screen to separate the juice. Centrifugal juicers may feature either a means of holding the pulp or of ejecting the pulp from an exit opening.

There are internal screw-type juicers, such as the Champion, that crush the fruits or vegetables pressed into them, then force the juice out by pressing the pulp against a heavy-duty, stainless-steel screen. This type of juicer also comes with a hydraulic press. One of the big advantages is that you can also use the screw-type juicer to make seed or nut butters, baby foods, and sorbets. Both personal and heavy-duty, commercial-grade Champion (screw-type) juicers are available.

Both the centrifugal and screw-type juicers clog up easily with soft fruit pulp or the pulp produced when juicing spinach or parsley. If you want to run spinach or parsley through a juicer the right way, work them into the rotating screw inside the machine by forcing them in with carrots or celery. You will get a mixed juice, but enriched by the chlorophyll-rich juice of the spinach or parsley.

Wheat grass juice, if you've ever encountered it in a health food store, is possibly the most expensive juice on the market. Made famous by the Hippocrates Health Institute in Florida, wheat grass juice is simply the green, chlorophyll-rich juice of young blades of wheat grass. Some people grow their own wheat grass in a window box or a plot in the garden. This grass is ground to pulp in a special type of heavy-duty, slow-turning juicer. The slower turning of the blade inside the juicer housing pulps the wheat grass without causing oxidation, and removes the green juice. High-speed juicers don't seem to handle spinach, grass, and other leaf-type green vegetables well at all. The green juices are used more for cleansing and may be the most appropriate juices for taking care of degenerative diseases.

WHY YOU SHOULD GET ON THE JUICE WAGON

We live in an age when hospital costs, doctors' fees, and many medical services are so high and disease statistics are so discouraging and overwhelming that it makes good sense to protect yourself as much as you can from diseases and other health disturbances.

Investigative research shows that many modern diseases are linked with nutrient deficiencies. Years of mineral deficiencies, for example, through poor or imbalanced food regimens, invite, encourage, and sustain chronic diseases. Fresh juices help prevent nutrient deficiencies.

How can diet-related deficiencies cause diseases? All body cells are programmed to use internal energy and externally provided nutrients (through the blood and interstitial fluid) to do their jobs in the body. But how can a cell do its job if it doesn't have the right kind of minerals to make its structure work right or to form the protein it was designed to make?

The answer is, it can't. Once a cell becomes weakened by mineral deficiencies (usually multiple), it becomes a pushover for various processes that may lead to DNA breakage in the cell nucleus, or to some other unfortunate malfunction. These breakdowns usually take place in cells that make up constitutionally weak tissues of the body, where only a slight malfunction can have terrible consequences, such as the initiation of degenerative diseases, including asthma, kidney failure, emphysema, cancer, or cardiovascular disease.

Juices are an effective measure and antidote for all health problems that begin with nutrient deficiencies. Juices have exactly the right ingredients for preventing or helping to reverse some diseases.

CHAPTER 4

GREENS IN YOUR JUICER

O ne of the great advantages of chlorophyll-rich juices is their cleansing effect on the bowel and other elimination systems, which results in a cleansing of the blood, lymph, and intracellular fluid. A clean body is an efficient body, a body that digests well, assimilates well, and is full of energy and vigor. Sickness and disease seldom gain a foothold in a clean, well-nourished body, or they leave when cleanliness is restored to a well-nourished body whose fatty tissues and inherently weak organs, glands, tissues, and systems are laced with catarrh, metabolic wastes, drug residues, and other contaminants.

In the preface to this book, I dramatized the healing power of green vegetable juice by describing my experience with the lady who had thirteen leg ulcers. After doctors in two prestigious clinics were unable to help her, "Dr. Chlorophyll" showed her that nature cures. When we begin to juice greens, we touch on the cleansing aspect of healing, a topic seldom discussed these days.

REMEDIAL EFFECTS OF CHLOROPHYLL

- Helps build a high blood count
- Counteracts toxins
- Helps purify the liver
- Feeds tissues magnesium
- Alleviates blood sugar problems
- Improves milk production
- Reduces or eliminates body odors
- Improves nasal drainage
- Relieves sore throat
- Soothes gastric ulcers
- Reduces catarrhal discharges
- Improves varicose veins
- Cleans and deodorizes bowel
- Soothes inflammation of some forms of hepatitis
- Supports blood coagulation in hemophilia
- Alleviates symptoms of asthma
- Helps sores heal faster
- Destroys bacteria in wounds
- Slows nasal drip
- Benefits inflamed lymph organs (tonsils, appendix, etc.)
- Soothes painful hemorrhoids
- Revitalizes vascular system
- Reduces pain caused by inflammation

There are several types of greens you may use in juicing, and I want to turn to the subject of how we juice greens for a moment before we continue with the topic of cleansing.

JUICING WITH GRASSES AND HERBS

I have seen many patients helped with green juices, which contain chlorophyll, enzymes, iron, magnesium, phosphorus, potassium, and sodium, as well as provitamin A, B-complex vitamins, and vitamins C, E, and K. The power of sunshine in chlorophyll is wonderfully cleansing in the body.

Green juices rich in potassium salts are supportive of heart function and neutralize muscle acids. Greens help protect the liver and gallbladder from the harmful effects of fats. The chlorophyll in greens cleanses the bowel and the bloodstream, and the provitamin A (carotene) has been demonstrated to be anticarcinogenic (protective against cancer).

Greens are rich in anticancer carotene, but so are carrots. As the story of my patient Del Wilhite attests (see chapter 2), carrots possess healing nutrients. Living on carrot juice for over a year had a positive impact on his bowel cancer. While he was fasting, I was amazed at what was passing from his bowel. In time, all his symptoms disappeared. Carrot juice is universally accepted by most people, while green juice from wheat grass, barley grass, alfalfa, or green, leafy vegetables must either be diluted with water or some milder juice or else sipped very slowly. Green juice is very potent, and most people have to be careful with it.

GREEN JUICE AND DEGENERATIVE DISEASE

The late Ann Wigmore, founder of the Hippocrates Health Institute, made raw wheat grass juice famous. She was a wonderful person, and I have the greatest respect for her work. She demonstrated that the nutritional effects of "live" raw foods and juices are often accompanied by a powerful reversal of disease and restoration of energy in those who have come to her institute for help.

H. E. Kirschner, M.D., mentioned in chapter 1, was another strong believer in the value of green juice. In the 1930s, Dr. Kirschner confirmed the healing value of green juice when he was in charge of two hundred tuberculosis patients at the Olive View Sanitorium near Los Angeles. He gave these patients a "green drink" daily containing pineapple juice, alfalfa, parsley, mint, spinach, herbs, dried kelp powder, almonds, dates, and sunflower seeds, all liquefied together in a blender. This drink was given as a supplement to their regular diet. Many patients gained weight, reported improved digestion and bowel function, and showed an increase in hemoglobin. Some patients considered terminal were out of bed and walking in six to eight months.

Here is his "green drink": Soak in water overnight fifteen almonds, four pitted dates, and 5 teaspoons sunflower seeds. In the morning, put these in a blender with presweetened pineapple juice and blend thoroughly. Then, take four large handfuls of greens (no stems), such as alfalfa, parsley, mint, spinach, beet greens, watercress, kale, chard, and herbs such as filaree, malva, lamb's quarter, and dandelion. Liquefy the greens in pineapple juice, then mix in the liquefied nuts, dates, and seeds and blend everything together. Doesn't that sound good?

Now, Dr. Kirschner's "green drink" was not a juice drink but a blended drink. Nevertheless, you can make a wonderful green juice drink using the same principles, and the directions follow.

Basic Green Juice: You may use wheat grass, barley grass, or alfalfa, but dilute with fresh parsley, mint, spinach, or even celery. Flavor with pineapple or apple juice, if you wish, or dilute with distilled water. To this basic, fresh, raw juice, you may add herbs—by juicing the fresh leaves, flowers, or roots; by adding the dried powder to the juice and mixing; or by making an herbal tea first, then mixing it with the basic green juice.

HERBAL TEAS DILUTED WITH JUICE

For a cooling summer drink for my patients and students, we often make up a big cooler of herbal tea mixed with juice. Herbal teas with distinctive pleasant flavors such as lemon grass or alfalfa-peppermint go well with apple juice, while other herbal teas go well with pineapple juice or blends of different fruit juices.

If you need an energy pickup, take a glass of any fruit or vegetable juice, add a heaping tablespoon of honeybee pollen, blend it for thirty seconds on high, and enjoy yourself. It tastes great and does good things for your energy.

MORE JUICE IDEAS AND THOUGHTS

When I was in the Swiss Alps in the 1930s at the Bircher-Benner Institute, founded by Dr. Max Benner in the 1890s, I watched researchers feed raw beets to laboratory rats. The beets successfully reduced the rate of cancer growth. Beets are cleansing for the liver, gallbladder, and bowel, and I always try to include a little beet juice or grated beet (the size of a golf ball) in my salads every day. I have had bowel troubles off and on all my life, and I give great credit to beets and beet juice for keeping me on the go.

I remember in the 1940s when Dr. Garnett Cheney at Stanford University discovered that raw green cabbage juice could heal peptic ulcers (*California Medicine*, 70 [1949]: 10–14). Juice half a head of green cabbage at a time and drink about a quart of cabbage juice over the course of a day. You can flavor the cabbage juice with celery or pineapple juice if you can't take it as it is. Some people find the cabbage juice a little too potent for their taste and prefer to take it diluted. Most peptic ulcer patients are cured within ten days of cabbage juice therapy.

In many cases of bleeding bowel, I have suggested that patients use green juice or liquid chlorophyll in their enema water. Chlorophyll has a soothing, cleansing, healing influence on the bowel.

Many years ago, a lady came to my health ranch in Escondido, California. She had a very limited, delicate gastrointestinal system due to over a hundred diverticula along one side of her colon. Her doctor wanted to surgically remove that section of her colon, but she came all the way to my ranch from back east, looking for an alternative. Almost all foods upset her digestion. I found one food that her digestive system tolerated very well: goat's milk. So I put her on a goat's milk diet. Milk, however, lacks iron and folic acid, so we had to add a little green juice to the milk to make sure she wouldn't get anemic. This lady stayed with me on my health ranch for over thirty years, working as an employee. I've never had a harder-working employee, although her diet consisted mainly of goat's milk with added chlorophyll. She also occasionally had certain fruits and a few nuts soaked overnight in apple juice as well as an egg yolk mixed with goat's milk.

ANOTHER WAY TO JUICE

If you can't afford to buy a juicer (you should be able to save up for one), you can make wheat grass or barley grass juice or juice from any other combination of greens by putting distilled water in a blender, adding handfuls of greens, and letting the blender chop them very fine. Pour into a crock or other large container and let soak two hours in a cool area. Then strain out the solids with cheesecloth or some other cloth, and you'll have your green drink—diluted, but still fresh, powerful, and loaded with chlorophyll.

DR. JENSEN'S DRINK

When I get tired or feel the need for an energy pickup, I ask for my drink. My friends and employees just call it "Dr. Jensen's Drink." The base is either goat's milk or soy milk (made with soy powder, *not* soy flour) and is mixed half-and-half with carrot juice or green juice. A teaspoon of almond butter or sesame seed butter and a teaspoon of some natural sweetener, such as honey, maple sugar, or date sugar, are added. On occasion, I ask for a sliver of avocado, a half banana, or a little beet juice to be added.

You may want to try it. Perhaps you'll add a touch of your own such as adding a few peppermint leaves to increase your own enjoyment, or add a particular nutrient that you know you need. That's the fun of juicing and making up blender drinks. You can get as creative as you want!

It is possible to purchase special slow-grinding juicers called wheat grass juicers, which press the juice from barley grass, wheat grass, alfalfa, sprouts, and other greens. But you can also juice greens in a fast screw-type juicer, if you juice them together with a hard vegetable such as carrots or celery. The hard vegetables give bulk or body to the soft greens, which give up their juice along with that of the harder vegetable.

This process of mixing hinders you from getting a pure green juice, but you will find the pure green juice so strong that you will be happy to dilute it. Remember, I didn't have a juicer when the woman with the thirteen leg ulcers came to me. I had her cut up all the leafy green vegetables by hand, and the juice was made by soaking the "minced" greens in distilled water. That made it mild and easy to drink. The leg ulcers cleared up, and she went back home.

HOW TO GROW WHEAT GRASS

Wheat grass not only contains an abundance of provitamin A and chlorophyll, it is rich in minerals and enzymes. It contains protein, prostaglandins, and trace elements. Because of its high nutritional value, some people like to grow it at home.

To grow wheat grass, soak wheat berries in water overnight and plant them the next morning in a tray or window box with at least an inch of moist mineral-rich dirt. Don't worry about making it deeper because you are going to harvest the wheat grass before it gets very high. Sprinkle the whole wheat berries on top of the soil in the box and sprinkle dirt on top of them until they are covered about ¼ inch deep. Water lightly each day, just enough to keep the soil damp. When the grass is 5 or 6 inches tall, cut it low and make juice out of it. (Ann Wigmore used to sprout her organic wheat berries first in a quart jar, then plant the sprouted berries.)

The pulp from wheat grass makes a wonderful poultice for drawing out the toxins in wounds, infections, boils, and cysts. If the need arises, place the pulp over the desired spot, cover with a moist cloth, then cover the moist cloth with a dry cloth or towel. The latter can be safety-pinned or velcro-fastened to hold the poultice on all night.

Of course, you can buy liquid chlorophyll made from alfalfa in most health food stores. It's good, but it isn't fresh.

Fresh green juice contains live enzymes, as do all raw foods, and those enzymes are the spark plugs that energize the hundreds of thousands of chemical reactions that go on in every living cell; every moment tearing down, building up, and changing one thing to another. An enzyme is a complex, active protein that is able to trigger a change in another substance without being changed itself. The more digestive enzymes we take in with juices and foods, the less energy our own bodies have to spend in processing and using our foods as they are broken down into elementary particles.

Freshly prepared green juices are sometimes used in programs to reverse chronic or degenerative diseases. Do they work? Along with a balanced diet, I would say they always help a great deal.

WHAT'S IN A GREEN JUICE?

When I talk about green juice, I'm covering a lot of territory. This includes dandelion greens, collard greens, mustard greens, beet greens, kale, spinach, chard, sprouts of many kinds, alfalfa, wheat grass, barley grass, turnip greens, watercress, parsley, cabbage, and asparagus. Green juices come from an impressive variety of sources, but they have many good things in common.

First of all, let's understand chlorophyll. Photosynthesis in the leaves of plants is a chemical powerhouse activated by sunlight to draw carbon dioxide from the air through the pores of the leaves. Chlorophyll is the green pigment in the leaves that absorbs sunlight and changes it into chemical energy. By splitting water molecules apart and recombining their hydrogen and oxygen with the carbon and oxygen of the carbon dioxide, carbohydrates are formed. All this takes place in the presence of chlorophyll. Carbohydrates are plant sugars or starches, some of which are stored in the roots or fruit of the plant, along with vitamins, minerals, enzymes, a little oil, a little protein, and a lot of water.

Chlorophyll is often called the "lifeblood" of plants, and the basic chlorophyll molecule is nearly identical to the hemoglobin molecule of the blood. The main difference is that there is an iron molecule in the center of the hemoglobin structure, while there is a magnesium molecule in the center of the chlorophyll molecule. Surprisingly, most green vegetables contain a milligram or two of iron per 100-gram portion in addition to the magnesium from the chlorophyll. Just to give you some idea of the quantity involved in a couple of different vegetables, 100 grams of raw parsley contains 6.2 milligrams of iron and 41 milligrams of magnesium, while 100 grams of watercress contains 1.7 milligrams of iron and 18.6 milligrams of magnesium. Adults need an average total intake of 18 milligrams of iron daily.

THE SECRET OF MY WORK

The secret of my work is building a high blood count in my patients, and nothing does better at building a good red blood cell count than green vegetable juices. A high red blood cell count means that more oxygen can be delivered to the tissues to aid in cellular respiration.

A third-generation vegetarian from Canada brought his daughter to me for help in correcting an anemic condition. She was a fourth-generation vegetarian, and had refused to take any animal-derived supplements. I gave her eight chlorophyll-rich drinks daily, and her red blood cell count rose from 2,800,000 to 3,800,000 in a month's time. When she left the ranch, her blood count was 4,500,000, almost normal. She regained her health and became very active and vigorous. She is married now, and her children are healthy and strong.

Vitamin K, the blood-clotting factor, is a fat-soluble vitamin found in all greens. All green vegetables, as well as carrot juice, are rich in vitamin A in the form of carotene. Science has proved that a diet high in carotene lowers the risk of cancer. Greens also contain from 50 milligrams to 100 milligrams of calcium per 100-gram serving, and most are high in potassium. There's a trace of copper and zinc in most greens.

Juice made from greens helps control calcium in the body, which assists in healing. It feeds the desirable bacteria and cleanses the bowel. It increases the blood-clotting ability as it builds up and cleanses the bloodstream. Experiments earlier in this century show that chlorophyll has antiseptic properties and is effective in disinfecting wounds. It is also a rejuvenating factor when used with a balanced diet. Green juices are a special gift from Mother Nature in detoxifying, cleansing, and restoring a polluted, run-down body.

SETTLING ON A RIGHT PROGRAM FOR LIVING

I want to point out that it isn't enough to drink a few glasses of fresh juice daily, hoping to compensate for poor eating habits and an unhealthy lifestyle. If you want to live a long, healthy life, you have to take a new path in life, and juices are only a small—though important—part of that new path.

A balanced diet, such as my Health and Harmony Food Regimen in chapter 1, is essential to a right way of living. Juices and other food supplements are used to "fine-tune" the diet to meet your individual needs. Regular exercise is another absolute necessity, along with adequate sleep and rest, and plenty of fresh air.

I love juices and what they do for my health, but I wouldn't have the health I possess at the age of ninety-one (as of this writing) if I hadn't followed a total health program, a path of right living.

FRIENDS FROM THE GARDEN AND FIELD

The following is a list of the finest green plants and vegetables for juicing that I know. Variety is a key to better health, so change the greens you use for juicing every few days.

Alfalfa. I recommend the use of fresh alfalfa in the basic green juice, not just as an additive, if you can get it fresh. Alfalfa is very deep-rooted, picking up trace elements such as zinc and silicon, as well as the calcium, magnesium, phosphorus, iron, and potassium, for which it is well known. Also included are sodium, sulfur, copper, manganese, cobalt, selenium, chloride, and iodine.

Use it for purifying the blood and for digestive problems. It also helps arthritis (use with chaparral), allergies, morning sickness, and the endocrine glands.

Alfalfa in the form of sprouts is one of the purest foods we can have for the body. Sprouts promote healthy bowel activity. Alfalfa in the form of tablets is helpful in keeping diverticula, bowel strictures, creases, and other parts of the intestine free of stagnant putrefactive materials. Alfalfa teas are alkaline and help maintain the blood acid/alkaline balance (pH 7.4).

Anise. This aromatic herb is often available in markets and health food stores in season and may be growing wild near your home. A little fresh anise in your green juice will reduce or eliminate gas formation in the stomach and bowel.

Beet Greens. Beet greens, containing potassium, magnesium, iodine, and iron, are an excellent body mineralizer. Clean and wash thoroughly. Use stems if they are tender. Beet greens juice is wonderful for the liver and gallbladder. A half glass per day will also help bowel movements.

Bok Choy. This Chinese cabbage is high in sulfur and iron, and is also high in potassium. Sulfur purifies and activates the body and is needed in proteins.

Brussels Sprouts. This member of the cabbage family is also high in sulfur. Many people find it gas-forming in a raw juice, so be cautious.

Cabbage. Cabbage juice is excellent for the stomach. It contains sodium, the youth element, which is stored there, and also potassium, the muscle toner. A medical doctor named Cheney from Stanford University cleared up ulcers of the stomach using cabbage juice as a remedy. Use raw cabbage in salads. There is almost as much vitamin C in a cup of raw cabbage as there is in half an orange.

Cayenne. I recommend adding a little powdered cayenne right in the juicer, no more than ½ teaspoon at first, for the circulation. Cayenne is good for the heart and blood pressure, for asthma and upper respiratory conditions, and to boost energy and endurance. You can use it with raw garlic (one or two cloves) to help lower blood pressure.

Celery Greens. Celery greens should be juiced along with the stalk. The potassium in the green tops balances the high sodium content of the stalk. If a person just takes the stalk, he will be getting a concentrated form of sodium. The overabundance of sodium causes water to be held in the body. An overabundance of potassium can also cause problems, but few people ever get too much potassium because our body requires so much of it. It specifically feeds the muscle structure, which makes up 80 percent of the solid portion of our body.

Chaparral. Like alfalfa, chaparral is a good blood cleanser and is especially effective juiced with other greens, providing a high-chlorophyll tonic to sweeten and cleanse the bowel. Chaparral is used most often for arthritis and degenerative conditions in the body.

Chives. These are high in potassium, calcium, and sulfur. Chives are good for catarrhal elimination.

Coriander (Cilantro). This wonderful culinary herb improves the taste of soups, salads, meat, fish, and poultry, and it also strengthens the heart and acts as a tonic to the digestive system. Juice a handful of fresh, green coriander in your green drink for a special lift.

Dandelion. Use the leaves and root if you want to cleanse the kidneys, liver, and gallbladder. This herb is also good for the bowel, spleen, and pancreas. A mild diuretic, it is good for anemia, diabetes, hypoglycemia, low blood pressure, and skin troubles. These greens are fine sources of calcium, manganese, chlorine, potassium, and iron.

Echinacea. This herb is a powerful detoxifying agent, and I recommend that it be made into a tea first by simmering in water for eight to ten minutes before adding to juice and mixing thoroughly. Purchase echinacea at a health food store and follow the directions concerning how much to add. This is one of the best cleansers for the lymph system, and good results have been obtained in some cases of degenerative disease.

Endive. While endive is bitter, it is also helpful in losing weight. Wash before juicing.

Escarole. Here is one of the greens that is most abundant in calcium. It also belongs to the sulfur family.

Malva. This wild weed is common throughout the United States and elsewhere in the world. One pound of fresh-picked malva has 50,000 units of natural vitamin A, which is so important in clearing up infections. Malva is tasty in salads and can be steamed like spinach. Be sure to clean the leaves first, using a teaspoon of chlorine bleach to a gallon of water. Soak the leaves for five minutes, then rinse thoroughly.

Nasturtium Flowers. These are another source of greens. Have them in salads.

Parsley. Parsley makes an outstanding chlorophyll drink for the kidneys. You can dry it for making parsley tea later. Use often in soups and broths. There is more iron in parsley than any other herb I know. It is high in provitamin A, a natural anticarcinogenic, and high in chlorophyll, nature's most powerful cleanser. Parsley is often available all winter long in the fresh vegetable department at your local market. Use it generously in making your green juice.

Parsley helps with kidney and gallstones, cleanses the liver, supports the heart, and is a good tonic for the blood vessels. Some report that it has helped their arthritis (all green herbs and leafy vegetables help reduce symptoms of arthritis, some better than others). Parsley is one of the few herbs that helps deodorize garlic or onion breath.

Peppermint, Spearmint, Mint. These herbs are high in chlorophyll. They make excellent flavorings for bitter drinks.
They are wonderful when it comes to driving gas out of
the intestinal tract and they also sweeten the interior
walls.

Sage. A potent herb I used to point out to my patients at the
health ranch on our morning walks. I'd tell them to pick
some, rub it in their hands, and smell it. Sage will open
your eyes and sinuses and wake up a sleepy head right
away.

A little sage added to your green drink will decrease
secretions of the mucous membranes, help with digestive
and bowel problems, reduce nervousness and night sweats,
expel parasites from the bowel, reduce morning sickness
and nausea, and help with skin problems. It is good to keep
in mind that sage may act as a sexual depressant in some
persons.

Spinach. Try to have a little bit in a raw juice, but do not
overdo it because it contains oxalic acid, which interferes
with the absorption of calcium in the body. Swiss chard
and beet greens also contain this acid—so does chocolate.
Considering the wide variety of greens in the garden,
spinach should be eaten or juiced about once a week.

Swiss Chard. A brother of the spinach, this family member is a
little more palatable than its kin. It also contains oxalic
acid.

Thyme. This popular cooking herb not only enhances flavor in
foods but is a strong stimulant for catarrhal elimination
from the upper respiratory system and an effective
headache remedy. It alleviates the symptoms of asthma and

hay fever, helps digestion, reduces flu discomfort and sore throat, and may help prevent kidney stones.

Watercress. This is one of the greatest of our garden friends for trimming off excess weight. Anyone overweight should consider getting more potassium and less sodium in the diet. This is a high-potassium food. Sodium holds water while potassium helps get rid of it.

Wheat Grass. This is one of the finest health builders I know. Wheat grass is high in indole, which helps prevent cancer, according to the National Academy of Sciences. It contains an enzyme (P4D1) that stimulates DNA repair if it has been damaged by chemicals. Wheat grass contains the enzyme superoxide dismutase (SOD), which neutralizes the worst free radicals (superoxides) and protects from cancer. Another important enzyme is catalase, which breaks down harmful hydrogen peroxide in the body and prevents it from harming cells. Catalase is abundant in wheat grass. (There are over twenty enzymes in wheat grass.) Wheat grass juice is abundant in provitamin A, chlorophyll, potassium, magnesium, and many other vitamins and minerals. According to the late V. E. Irons, who was an early advocate of radical detoxification to prevent and reverse disease, the only nutrients it lacks are vitamins D and B_{12}.

Fresh herbs are not as potent as the dried, powdered herbs, or herbal teas, decoctions, or extracts (alcohol-dissolved herbal essences). Like other live nutrients, they are among nature's whole, pure, and natural foods. Their fresh juice adds the special healing touch found only in herbs.

For a special taste treat, add fresh lemon grass, spearmint, peppermint, or licorice to green juice sweetened with fresh, natural pineapple juice.

Herbs commonly found fresh at the supermarket these days (in season) include coriander, parsley, lemon grass, tarragon, mint, sage, marjoram, rosemary, oregano, thyme, basil, anise, garlic, and chives. Some of these are primarily used in cooking, while others have distinctive healing value as well.

This list is by no means complete but is intended as a reminder of some of the valuable foods we have in the garden. I hope you begin using them, if you are not already doing so.

CHAPTER 5

BEST FRUITS AND VEGETABLES FOR JUICING

I believe we should use juices according to season, just as we use the ripe fruits and vegetables according to season, with some commonsense deviations. Where winters are cold, and ice and snow rule out any homegrown fruit or vegetables, you may use what you find available in the stores, or reconstitute dried fruit by soaking overnight, starting with boiling water. I urge you, however, to follow nature's law of variety in foods by also using a variety of juices in all seasons of the year. Don't just have the same juice or juice combination every day.

Variety in what we eat and drink is the only real insurance we can get to make sure our bodies are getting all the chemical elements and nutrients we need.

Because vitamin B_{12} is so necessary, yet so lacking in fruits and vegetables, I advise adding a couple of grams of chlorella to your juice twice a day, blending it in your blender. Chlorella is an edible alga, loaded with nutrients, very high in vitamin

B_{12}, as well as in the nucleic factors that help us stay young and in a "growth factor" that stimulates healing. You can't go wrong in making this addition. Chlorella is available in most health food stores.

Vegetables keep longer than fruits because they have lower sugar and moisture content. For the same reason, many of the soft fruits—if they are fully ripe—are almost as quickly and easily digested and assimilated as fruit juices. It is harder to juice soft fruits, however, because the soft pulp keeps clogging the straining portion of the juicers. For this reason, some soft fruits, such as peaches or apricots, are better tossed in the blender and processed into "nectars."

All juices should be used within six hours after they are made, but preferably within one hour.

ANALYTICAL FOOD GUIDE

On the following pages, I have included Table 5.1, my Analytical Food Guide, to assist you in selecting the fruits and vegetables for juicing and liquefying. This table includes the food and type, predominant chemical elements, the best way to prepare and serve for good digestion, and the remedial measures.

This table will aid your selection of foods for any particular health requirements. I hope you will find the information to be very helpful, as it has proven to be a valuable tool in my work for many years.

Table 5.1. Analytical Food Guide

Food & Type	Predominant Chemical Elements	Best Way Prepared and Served for Digestion	Remedial Measures
Almonds (Carbohydrate)	Potassium, Phosphorus, Magnesium	Serve with vegetables or fruit. Almonds, celery, apple: a complete meal. Make almond nut milk drink.	Muscle, brain, nerve food. Best of nuts to use. Good source of fiber; no cholesterol.
Apples (Carbohydrate)	Potassium, Phosphorus, Magnesium	Eat alone, in salads, or with proteins. Juice or blend.	Skins used for tea. Very low in fat. Fine for kidney/urinary tract. High in insoluble fiber. Good for bowel and liver regulators.
Apricots (Carbohydrate)	Potassium, Calcium, Iron	Use only fresh or dried (unsulfured), alone or in salads. Juice or blend them.	Good for anemia, constipation, and catarrh.
Artichokes (Carbohydrate)	Potassium, Phosphorus, Calcium	Steam as cooked vegetable. Good cold or hot.	Good for soft bulk, minerals, and as general body builder and immunity builder.

(Continued)

Table 5.1. **Continued**

Food & Type	Predominant Chemical Elements	Best Way Prepared and Served for Digestion	Remedial Measures
Asparagus (Sulfur)	Potassium, Phosphorus, Calcium	Cut up fine and steam. Juice or blend.	Good for kidney/bladder disorders.
Avocado (Carbohydrate, Fat)	Potassium, Magnesium, Iron	Eaten alone or in salads and soups. Use as vegetable dip or sandwich filling. Blend to make drinks and dressings.	Body builder. Good for colitis, ulcers. Use as natural oil and intestinal bulk. Slightly laxative. Good mineralizer for body.
Banana (Carbohydrate)	Potassium, Magnesium, Phosphorus	Eat alone or in salads. Starch; eat dead-ripe, in drinks, or baked.	Good for gaining weight. Natural bulk for bowel conditions such as colitis, ulcers, or diarrhea. Low fat.
Barley (Carbohydrate, Protein)	Potassium, Phosphorus, Calcium	Starch; use alone or in soups.	Good for gaining weight. Good source for silicon.
Bass (Protein)	Potassium, Phosphorus, Sodium	Broil, bake, or steam.	Brain, nerve food. Good broth for nerves and glands.

Food	Minerals	Preparation	Benefits
Beans, Lima (Carbohydrate, Protein)	Potassium, Phosphorus, Sodium	Steam or use in vegetable/protein loaves. Cook and juice for many combinations.	Puree for stomach ulcers. Muscle-building food.
Beans, String (Carbohydrate, Protein)	Potassium, Calcium, Phosphorous	Steam or juice.	Good body mineralizer.
Beef (Protein)	Potassium, Phosphorus, Sodium	Broil or roast. Serve with green vegetables and tomatoes or grapefruit.	Brain and nerve food. Good for anemia.
Beets (Carbohydrate)	Potassium, Phosphorus, Sodium	Steam, also shred/steam. Juice.	Juice combined with blackberry juice is good blood builder. Best juice for gallbladder and liver problems. Laxative in effect.
Beet Greens (Carbohydrate)	Potassium, Calcium, Magnesium	Steam like spinach. Juice (take only small amounts).	Body mineralizer.

(Continued)

Table 5.1. **Continued**

Food & Type	Predominant Chemical Elements	Best Way Prepared and Served for Digestion	Remedial Measures
Blackberries (Carbohydrate)	Potassium, Calcium, Magnesium	Serve with other fruit, protein, or alone. Juice.	Blood builder. Used for diarrhea and anemia.
Blueberries (Carbohydrate)	Potassium, Calcium, Phosphorus	Serve with other fruit, protein, or alone. Juice.	Blood purifier, body mineralizer.
Bread, Whole Wheat (Carbohydrate, Protein)	Sodium, Potassium, Phosphorus	Serve once a day with raw vegetable juice, salads.	Good for teeth, muscles, bones, and anemia.
Broccoli (Carbohydrate)	Potassium, Calcium, Phosphorus	Steam, juice, or blend.	Body mineralizer.
Brussels Sprouts (Sulfur)	Potassium, Phosphorus, Calcium	Steam or blend.	Good mineralizer.
Butter, Cow (Fat)	Potassium, Calcium, Phosphorus	Serve on toast, vegetables in moderation. Use sweet butter.	Supplies vitamin A; good for eyes. Easiest fat to digest.

Buttermilk (Protein)	Potassium, Magnesium, Calcium	Serve with citrus fruit or protein. Juices can be added.	Good for diarrhea, gas normalizer, acidity.
Cabbage (Carbohydrate)	Potassium, Calcium, Phosphorus	Boil, use raw in salad, or juice. Reported to help stomach ulcers.	Good mineralizer.
Carrots (Carbohydrate)	Potassium, Calcium, Phosphorus	Finely shred for salads, raw, or steamed. High in beta-carotene. Mildest juice. Mixes well with other juices.	Good for eyes, hair, nails, teeth, jaws. Use to break fasts.
Casaba (Carbohydrate)	Potassium, Phosphorus, Calcium	Eat like other melons; fill center with berries. Juice is wonderful.	Blood cleanser; cooler.
Cauliflower (Carbohydrate)	Potassium, Phosphorus, Calcium	Steam.	Good intestinal cleanser.
Celery (Carbohydrate)	Potassium, Calcium, Phosphorus	Best eaten raw or juice; steam; blend.	For arthritis, neuritis, rheumatism, acidity, high blood pressure, nerves. Blood cleanser.

(Continued)

Table 5.1. **Continued**

Food & Type	Predominant Chemical Elements	Best Way Prepared and Served for Digestion	Remedial Measures
Chayote (Carbohydrate)	Potassium, Magnesium, Calcium	Steam. Good as juice also.	Nonfattening and good mineralizer.
Cheese, Cottage (Cow) (Protein)	Sodium, Phosphorus, Potassium	Eaten as protein. Always serve with fruit or vegetables.	Good source of complete protein.
Cheese, Cottage (Goat) (Protein)	Phosphorus, Chlorine, Calcium	Always serve with fruit or vegetables.	Abundance of fluorine. Good for bones, teeth, beauty. Especially good for children.
Cheese, Roquefort (Goat) (Protein)	Sodium, Calcium, Phosphorus	Always serve with fruit or vegetables.	Abundant in fluorine. Good for bones and teeth.
Cheese, Swiss (Cow) (Protein)	Calcium, Phosphorus, Chlorine	Always serve with fruit or vegetables.	Good body builder.

Food	Minerals	Serving	Benefits
Cherries, Sweet Raw (Carbohydrate)	Potassium, Calcium, Phosphorus, Iron	Serve with protein or alone. Juice or blend.	For anemia, catarrh, chronic gallbladder trouble.
Chervil (Carbohydrate)	Potassium, Phosphorus, Magnesium	Eat with salads, vegetables, proteins, carbohydrates. Add a little juice to other juices.	Body mineralizer.
Chicken (Protein)	Potassium, Phosphorus, Sodium	Serve with nonstarch vegetables, tomatoes, or grapefruit.	Tissue building and repair.
Chinese Cabbage (Carbohydrate)	Potassium, Calcium, Phosphorus	Raw in salad or prepare as other varieties of cabbage.	Body mineralizer.
Chives (Carbohydrate)	Potassium, Calcium, Phosphorus	Use in salads, other vegetables, or cottage cheese.	Body mineralizer good for catarrh.
Coconut (Protein, Fat)	Potassium, Phosphorus, Magnesium	Milk and coconut meat eaten with fresh or diced fruit or vegetables.	Body builder/weight builder. Good for bones, teeth.

(Continued)

Table 5.1. **Continued**

Food & Type	Predominant Chemical Elements	Best Way Prepared and Served for Digestion	Remedial Measures
Corn (Carbohydrate, Protein)	Potassium, Phosphorus, Calcium	Steam cobs; eat with green vegetables.	Great brain, bone, muscle-building food.
Cranberries (Carbohydrate)	Potassium, Calcium, Phosphorus	Not recommended to eat. Too high in oxalic acid.	Use as pack in rectum for treating hemorrhoids. Juice for urinary tract cleansing.
Cream, Cow (Fat)	Potassium, Calcium, Phosphorus	Eat with fruit or vegetables.	Weight builder.
Cucumbers (Carbohydrate)	Potassium, Phosphorus, Calcium	Serve in salads, with starch or protein. Good as juice in summer drinks.	Cools blood; good for skin trouble.
Currants, Black (Carbohydrate)	Potassium, Calcium, Phosphorus	Currant juice is refreshing.	Blood builder.

about your life and career. A business reporter might be more interested in how you rose through the ranks, from slinging envelopes in the mailroom to becoming a chief executive; on the other hand, a style section reporter may be more interested in how growing up as the son of a Marine captain shaped your values. As an introvert, you might be most comfortable anticipating the types of questions you'll be asked, and then rehearsing them. Plan for the usual *who, what, where, when, why,* and *how* questions. Also plan for questions that come out of left field, such as, "Why were you wearing a Hawaiian shirt and a pith helmet at the meeting?" The trick is to be flexible enough to handle questions you don't think you'll be asked, and practicing answers to gain confidence.

2. Be concise. Let's say a friend asked you what you did this morning. You might say, "I woke up at 7 a.m., rubbed my eyes, got out of bed slowly, went to the bathroom, splashed some water on my face, and spotted a pink elephant sunning on my lawn." If it's a press interview, all you need to say is, "I spotted a pink elephant sunning on my lawn." That's editing, and that's what's newsworthy. If it's not a live interview, reporters will have control over what they use from you and how they use it—if at all. They're often under very tight deadlines. Keep your answers under 30 seconds; they'll be more likely to use them—and call you again. Introverts: Practice is essential. Get a stop watch and time yourself giving a brief response.

3. Know your audience. Ask the reporter who the story is targeting and then tailor your remarks. Wouldn't your language be different when addressing a group of fifth graders than a group of rocket scientists? Also, avoid industry jargon to save reporters from asking you for clarification. Tell a reporter why something is significant and why the audience should care in simple, straightforward language.

4. Answer the question you're asked. Too often people—especially politicians—answer the question they want asked rather than the question that is asked. Use your introvert's propensity to listen carefully. Others may have advised you to do the opposite and to make your message heard, regardless of what the reporter wants or needs. That's wasting a reporter's time. No reporter wants to keep asking the same question several different ways to get an answer—especially on a live interview. That reporter will surely not call you again. When you listen to the questions, chances are you'll be able to work your talking points into the answers. Often at the end of an interview, reporters will ask if there's anything else you'd like to add. That's your opportunity to bring up something you haven't yet covered.

5. Be relaxed. Introverts usually aren't crazy about speaking impromptu. If you're tense, chances are you'll speak too fast, you won't breathe normally, your voice will sound strained, and your pitch may even go up. Also, don't speak in a monotone. The more natural your voice sounds, the more likely you'll get airtime on radio or TV as well as capture the attention of a newspaper reporter who's asking you questions.

6. Never read from a press release. They're not meant to be read out loud. Practice delivering your message conversationally. Audio- or video-tape yourself to fine-tune your delivery.

7. Be engaged. Close your office door and turn your phone off so you won't be distracted during the interview. If you're interviewed in person, maintain eye contact with the reporter. Be personable and passionate, even if it's the tenth time you've told the same anecdote.

8. Be nonconfrontational. Don't snap at your interviewer. Years ago, I had the misfortune of asking a legendary jazz singer a perfectly innocuous question that she didn't like. She was easily in her seventies at the time, and I certainly had no reason to grill her.

She snapped at me, and the interview, which lasted only a minute or so longer, quickly went downhill. She got away with it because she was an icon. However, I don't recommend that you do it. If you snap or lose your temper, it might make great theater, but you could damage your reputation and credibility.

9. Offer facts and figures. Journalists love statistics, but make them brief and easily understandable. That will give your stats a better chance of being used.

10. Call right back. Keep in mind that reporters are often under tight deadlines. Always call them back as soon as possible. If they don't hear from you, sometimes within minutes, they'll move on to someone else.

TV Interviews

Michele Wucker, executive director of the World Policy Institute, a global think tank, shares what it was like for her, as an introvert, to appear on live national TV. "In a weird way," she notes, "the awkward setup that most TV interviews entail is actually good for introverts. You're alone in a little room with an earpiece in your ear and a little camera in front of you, behind a closed door."

Public Speaking

Public speaking is an efficient way for an introvert to raise her or his visibility. If it sounds like a frightening means to an end, it doesn't have to be. Help is available; you can conquer your fear of public speaking with the right support. I developed my public speaking skills by doing pro bono presentations, and after a short while, I was able to charge a fee. I got elected to boards of directors at professional organizations—volunteer positions that enabled me to develop strong relationships for mutual referrals, collaborations, valuable information, and more speaking opportunities. You don't have to do stump speeches to qualify as a public speaker. Start small and see where it takes you. For a more in-depth discussion on public speaking and presentation skills, see Chapter 6.

Writing

While writing doesn't come easily to me, I like that I can edit privately, on my own time. It's a safe way to communicate for an introvert. Getting published, whether it's in a newsletter, a book, or a blog, is a smart way to benefit many people by sharing your expertise while also raising your visibility.

David Vinjamuri, author of *Accidental Branding*, says: "Writing enhances your personal brand by positioning you as an expert. Writing a book has had multiple downstream benefits for me. I've gotten a lot more speaking engagements and media coverage. I'm also now writing regularly for *Brandweek*, I'm a regular guest on *Fox Business News*, and I've gotten new clients."

Kathleen Waldron, Ph.D., president of Baruch College, offers a creative idea: "Early in my career, I went to a senior person and we cowrote a one-pager for one of the trade journals. I did most of the work and he worked on it also, but it was clearly a coauthorship. It really was very self-promoting for me to do it, and in a non-threatening way. Of course, I linked my name to a more senior person's—and he and I just traded career opportunities. I helped him, he helped me, and we're still in touch 20 years later."

Op-Eds

Op-eds are perfect for anyone who likes to think, write, and express her views; they're also a great way to raise your visibility. So they're ideal for introverts. Several women I know have enthusiastically recommended The OpEd Project; its Web site (www. theopedproject.org) says that it "trains women experts across the nation to project their voices on the op-ed pages of major newspapers and other key forums of public discourse." According to Catherine Orenstein, the founder of The OpEd Project, women tend to shy away from claiming to be experts. My experience working with introverts—women and men alike—is similar. We often undersell how much we know. While women can directly benefit from The OpEd Project and its sister resource, www.SheSource. org, which is a repository of women experts, any introvert can get inspired by the idea and write an op-ed.

Referrals

As a coach, much of my business is through referrals. I take care of my clients, and they spread the word for me. I also get referrals from friends, colleagues, and former managers. What are your sources of referrals? Who can write letters of recommendation and testimonials for your promotional materials?

Social Media

Social media offer additional possibilities for you to expand your horizons while sitting at your computer. Blogs, message boards, wikis, and Yahoo! and Google groups enable you to write to people and share ideas; podcasts and YouTube let you broadcast your message to a potentially large audience; and social networking sites, like LinkedIn, Facebook, and Twitter, let you share information and stay informed. Of course, sites can gain massive popularity almost overnight, so watch for new ones that may crop up.

We'll discuss how you can use social media to raise your visibility in the pages that follow. Meanwhile, if you're just getting up the learning curve, check out the fun and instructive YouTube video titled "LinkedIn in Plain English" (there are also videos for Twitter, wikis, and RSS) created by Lee LeFever and Sachi LeFever—their Web site is www.commoncraft.com.

Introverts and Our Keyboards

"Studies are finding that introverts are a significant force behind the emergence of social media, including blogs, social networks, and other user-generated content," says Rick Lavoie, senior account director at Critical Mass, a digital marketing agency. Many of us prefer to spend more time sitting at our keyboards than interacting face-to-face. Online interactions not only enable us to gather our thoughts, take the time to edit, and share our ideas when we're ready; they also help us reach many more people than we'd have energy for when working a room, pounding the pavement, or even making cold calls. While face-to-face and online approaches to marketing yourself are not mutually exclusive, it's easier for us introverts to rely more on digital media to get the job done.

Which of the digital media do you gravitate to for your various communication needs? How about your audiences? "Talking has become a rarity," says a client of mine we'll call Genevieve Menard, an executive assistant at an investment bank. "In the Midtown sky-scraper where I work, I run into corporate lawyers, marketing executives, and financial executives every day. They're busy look-ing down at their BlackBerrys and cell phones whenever they step out of the office. Even their secretaries have BlackBerrys. On most mornings I'm greeted by silence when I step into the packed eleva-tor." So as a nation, we're becoming all thumbs!

How do we spread our message and raise our visibility using digital media? "It's not about driving people to your Web site any-more. Instead, it's about engaging in conversations with your audi-ence by blogging, generating content on sites such as YouTube, and social networking on sites such as LinkedIn. Your audiences will not only become aware of you. They'll also see the value of your contributions," says Lavoie. So introverts, our time has come!

Who's Watching

Just as you would in traditional networking situations, consider the image you want to get across in the arena of social networking. Maintaining a professional presence on social networking sites can give you an edge over the competition when you're seeking a job. A nationwide CareerBuilder.com survey of more than 3,100 employers found that 22 percent of hiring managers use social networking sites to research candidates, and an additional 9 percent plan on doing so. Furthermore, of those who researched candidates on these sites, 24 percent found content that helped solidify their decision to hire the candidate, and 34 percent found content causing them to dismiss the candidate from consideration. Top areas of concern included candidates' posting information about their drinking or using drugs (41 percent), posting provocative or inappropriate photographs or information (40 percent), exhibiting poor communication skills (29 percent), bad-mouthing their previous company or fellow employee (28 percent), lying about qualifications (27 percent), and making discriminatory remarks related to such characteristics as race, gender, or religion (22 percent). Other faux pas included using an unprofessional screen name, being linked to criminal behavior, and sharing confidential information from previous employers.[3] Can you believe?

So now that it's clear that you'll only put your best foot forward on the likes of LinkedIn, how can you help recruiters and hiring managers—who comprise 27 percent of LinkedIn subscribers—as well as prospective clients, find you?[4] Peter Engel, a senior recruiter with Cantor Executive Search Solutions, which specializes in the public relations industry, says that he particularly likes using LinkedIn for getting the most up-to-date information on candidates. He mainly uses keywords (e.g., social media, health care, business to business, crisis communications, writer, agency, broadcast) when searching for candidates.

"LinkedIn helps me connect the dots from prospective candidates to people whose reputations I know of. For example, if I look up a job candidate and see that the person has 50 connections, the chances are pretty good that I'll know 5 percent of them either directly or by reputation. If I see Jane Smith at XYZ Agency on LinkedIn, I might say, 'Oh yeah, I remember her. Is she still there?'

"From there," he continues, "I will reach out to Jane with a specific reason in mind. I will soon know whether Jane is working, looking for a job, or might be attractive for a position I'm looking to fill.

Whether Jane is interested in that particular job or not, I've made contact and added her updated résumé to my database. If she's looking for a job in a few months, she's top of mind. It's a way for everyone to win." LinkedIn is also a useful tool for researching companies and identifying who in your professional network is connected to someone in those companies. Let the introductions begin!

Your Online Social Network

Howard Greenstein, a social media strategist and evangelist, and president of the Harbrooke Group consultancy, talks about how you can use social media to increase your visibility and build your network: "Social networking sites enable you to connect with people you went to college with or worked with in previous jobs. Many can alert you to the presence of people from companies you list in your employment history. These people can see what you've done and when you change your employment status."

He offers an example: "So if you've been promoted from associate to vice president, the site will alert your network, and people can get in touch. This can help build your prominence in your career. Another nice feature is that as you build your network, you can send questions to your contacts. And when people in your network pose questions, you can answer them. If your answers are well regarded, people can rate them. The more people who rate you on providing answers on a particular topic, the more likely you'll get a little badge that says you're an expert." Greenstein describes more of the potential benefits: "So it can actually bring you accolades just by participating in this kind of conversation. You can also find jobs and opportunities on these sites."

Advice for Newcomers to Social Media

Greenstein offers advice to social media newcomers: "First, try out some of the social networks with a few trusted people—maybe a techie or a frequent user. Ask them to invite you into their online networks. That way, you can build up your network slowly and get used to the site. Read the help section. Many of these sites have a blog where you can learn what the leaders of the company are thinking about and what features they're adding."

As much as I love the unlimited potential of the Web, I have mixed feelings about some aspects of social networking. The main reason I'm not more active on social networking sites is that I'm private by nature and not comfortable with, in effect, sharing the names of my contacts with anyone who cares to inquire. So if someone I know invites me to join her network, I usually agree. However, I don't actively invite people to join my network—and certainly not my coaching clients, many of whom don't want it to be known that they're working with a coach. You may have similar concerns or you may just want to expand your network through other Internet options, such as blogs and podcasts, both of which we'll discuss now with Greenstein.

Blogs

"I marvel at how blogs have completely shifted the landscape of how everyone from sole proprietors to news media to major corporations can communicate with their constituents in a more informal and timely way," says Greenstein. "The important part of a blog is the ability for readers to leave comments in an interactive format. That back-and-forth communication builds the blog community." He continues: "Blogs also let other Web sites—especially search engines—know when new content is available. So when you publish a new blog entry, most blog software will send off a little 'ping' notice to Google, Yahoo!, and other big search engines to say: 'Hey, there's new content here.' Usually in 10 to 15 minutes your new content is indexed and available to people searching for it. It's an opportunity for you to share your opinions and create a human presence, especially if you're a small to mid-sized business."

Adds Senia Maymin, publisher and editor in chief of the daily news site PositivePsychologyNews.com: "Of our 30 plus authors, at least a quarter have their own blogs and newsletters. The best thing for an introvert about running a blog is that it's interaction on your own terms, on your own time, and it doesn't feel pressured by the readers. You set the agenda. You can decide what time of day you want to interact." (I like that we can now all be citizen journalists. The downside of the blogosphere is the unevenness of quality out there. However, that varies in traditional media as well.)

Greenstein talks about how you can benefit by creating your own blog: "Publishing a blog can help you build your business by telling people what you care about, how you do business, your customer service philosophy, anecdotes of how you've served customers, and products that you recommend. Also, most people who run a business have a Web site that's static, like a brochure. Since it doesn't change often, there's little reason for people to come back after they've seen it once. In contrast, blog content can change constantly." Greenstein mentions some useful resources: "Books I recommend on blogging include *Naked Conversations* by Robert Scoble and Shel Israel and *Now Is Gone* by Geoff Livingston and Brian Solis."

Podcasts

If you'd rather speak than write, podcasts are a simple way for you to get out your message. In case you've heard of podcasts but still aren't sure exactly what they are, here's how Greenstein describes them: "A podcast is a digital media file distributed over the Internet for playback on a portable media player or a personal computer." He adds: "It's effectively a radio program on the Net made by an amateur or a pro. The difference between a podcast and an audio download is that you can subscribe to a podcast, and every time it's updated, it can appear on your computer or in your media player. Like a magazine, 'subscriptions' is the word we use, but typically, there is no cost to get a podcast.

"Audio podcasts can sound pretty professional with just a $70 microphone setup," notes Greenstein. "Lots of services will host your podcast for free. They often put an advertisement at the beginning or the end of your podcast as the quid pro quo trade-off. There are also other services that will host your podcasts for a fixed monthly amount. Blog Talk Radio lets you do a podcast using only your telephone!" Some self-promoters go a step further by grabbing their video cameras and posting their videos to YouTube. "But," Greenstein warns, "videocasts aren't so easy to create. They can look amateurish and unprofessional if they're not well considered." He continues: "To learn more about podcasting, attend Podcamp events, which are free or inexpensive conferences held all over the world (www.podcamp.org), or read *Tricks of the Podcasting Masters* by Rob Walsh and Mur Lafferty."

Our ability to go inward and concentrate before we take action is one of the gifts that we often take for granted as introverts. In this chapter you picked your self-promotion goals, you created a marketing mix of the activities you handpicked to get you there, and you either built or considered (if you're not much of a planner) a personalized game plan that makes the best use of your time and money. So now, rather than sending you out on "Mission: Impossible," you're well equipped with the tools to build your empire (or just make a few calls).

Which leads us to Chapter 4. Imagine someone trying to sell you the best prime rib on the planet—and you're a vegetarian. Or pressuring you to join the local parent-teachers association—and you don't have kids. Self-promoting or selling always involves at least two parties—for simplicity, let's call them a buyer and a seller. You can save yourself so much scrambling and guesswork by learning about your target audiences, or the people who are most likely to be a match for your offerings. As always, we'll go inward to see what you can learn using your quiet strengths. I hope you enjoy the discovery process. Ready?

REFLECTIONS AND ACTIONS

What You Learned

1. _____

_____

2. _____

_____

3. _____

_____

Action: What will you do?	How You'll Do It: What support or further information will you obtain?	Accountability: Whom will you tell about this action?	Completion Date: By when?

four

Your Target Audiences

Going Inward and Reaching Outward

Your target audiences have needs and wants, and you have plenty to offer. In this chapter we'll look at the overlap between what they want and what you've got. Your target audiences are anyone you want to reach: your boss, your colleagues, your clients and prospects, your mentors, people who can recommend you or connect you to opportunities, those who read your blog, and so on. While it may sound daunting to appeal to all these stakeholders, you can do so well by using your introvert's propensities for researching, quietly analyzing ways to reach them, offering expertise they will value, writing information that will interest them, and building deep, lasting relationships with them.

You already have extensive experience as a target audience—for everything from life insurance to car repairs. People are trying to sell you stuff every day, and you can't possibly buy it all. What makes you buy what you buy? Chances are you go for what you need or want. Simply put, you'll buy whatever answers the question that advertisers broadcast on the fictional yet popular commercial-only radio station What's In It For Me?—or WIIFM. It's not a new concept, and it's basic, yet it's easy to forget. So I'll remind you of it periodically.

Before we go further into the heads of those you'll target, we'll look at what goes through *your* head when someone tries to sell you something or promote herself to you. Not to say that your target audience necessarily thinks the way you do; however, this can be a useful starting point. Along the same lines, in this chapter we'll explore your hiring decisions to gain insights about why people would hire you. Ultimately, you'll find a way of promoting yourself that honors both you and your target audiences. No need to do anything embarrassing or beneath you. Much of what we'll cover in this chapter overlaps with the chapters on networking, public speaking, and interviewing. However, here we'll zero in on targeting your audiences, which is essential to your success at all of those self-promotion activities.

YOU, YOU, YOU

I have a mantra to help you whenever you think of promoting yourself: You, you, you. Certainly, when I'm on the buying side of the equation and the seller makes everything about me, me, me, my WIIFM kicks in and the seller can engage me with minimal effort. And so it follows that when I'm the one wearing the seller's hat, my mantra reminds me to focus on my target audience—to ultimately reach them, them, them.

This mantra affects the way I do business, even in small ways. For example, I usually start e-mails and phone conversations with a line or two about the other person—inquiring about her latest news, congratulating him on his promotion, or referring to our last exchange. I get to why I'm touching base quickly—but not without first showing interest in the other person. Starting with an open-ended question (hint: they often start with *who, what, where, when, why,* or *how*) is particularly helpful for us introverts because it gets our conversation partners talking while we take our time warming up. What mantra can remind you whom to focus on when you're promoting yourself?

PITCHING AND RECEIVING PITCHES

While I certainly wasn't born to sell (anything, including myself), I often find being sold to even more unwelcome. Even though I know better on a conscious level, when I think of selling or being sold to, the first few words that come to my introverted mind are: *invading, pushing,* and *stretching the truth*. Clearly, I'm not alone in my bias: Development Dimensions International (DDI), a global talent management consultancy, found that 46 percent of corporate buyers surveyed across six countries (Australia, Canada, France, Germany, the United Kingdom, and the United States) said that they would not be proud to call themselves salespeople. The buyers most commonly described their perceptions of the sales process as "a necessary evil." Worse, colorful descriptions they used to describe salespeople included "irritating, like a rash you want to scratch but your doctor won't let you," "leeches," and "they come, they lie, they steal, they go."[1] Do you have biases about salespeople that make you leery about selling? If you see salespeople as slick or condescending purveyors of useless products who sneer at your questions, then how do you justify selling—including selling yourself—without feeling like a phony?

A client of mine we'll call Maria Maldonado, an international banker and specialist in Latin American economic affairs, offers her insights about the different ways that introverts and extroverts approach selling. "I've seen two kinds of selling," she says. "One kind is the banker who builds relationships that deepen in time. People who are more introverted do well with these one-on-one encounters. The other is the product people that the banker calls in to ask, for example: 'Can you sell Treasury or foreign exchange services to this client?' The product salespeople parachute in, give a presentation to sell their product, and parachute out." She points out: "That's much harder for an introvert because it doesn't entail relationship building."

Maldonado goes on to say, "If you're more introverted, selling is much easier when you have passion. I always believe in what I'm selling and give a lot of thought about the impact of my banking products on my clients. I get clear about the specifics of how I can help them, and that helps convince them. When you gain good clients, they give you business, you get more opportunities, and you gain visibility in your industry. That helps you to the next step." She concludes with an encouraging reminder: "One success builds on the other."

You don't have to make grand gestures or launch major media campaigns to effectively target your audiences. Sometimes, small, memorable actions are all it takes. Think of the last time someone promoted herself successfully to you. Chances are you felt engaged rather than bamboozled because the self-promoter solved a problem, addressed a need, provided you a shortcut, or otherwise delivered something that you were interested in. She listened to you and helped you to visualize a solution. You were so absorbed that you might not have even noticed that she was trying to sell you something. In effect, you were on the same side of the table.

How Google Stepped into the Shoes of Its Target Audience

More than 10 years ago, Web sites with flashy banner ads proliferated on the Web. Many went bust because Web advertising wasn't that effective. Then Google came along and offered a top-notch search capability coupled with a simple but brilliant idea—that when people are searching for something, they may also be interested in buying items related to it. Google sold simple text ads with no flash and became immediately profitable. The brains at Google put themselves in the shoes of their target audience and delivered what people who conduct searches wanted. The rest is history.

YOU AND YOUR TARGET AUDIENCES

Now let's talk about your target audiences, or the people who need or want what you have to offer. It may come as a relief to realize that they're probably only a tiny sliver of the population, rather than "el mundo." The clearer you are about who is in that sliver and what you can offer that they'll care about, the better you can target them. Gaining this clarity can help you focus your efforts, rather than waste your energy—a precious resource for an introvert—trying to please everyone. Envision yourself as a problem solver for a specific segment of the population, rather than as a glad-handing lounge lizard.

Let's do an exercise to help you think further about your target audience. You can write in the target audiences you identified in Chapter 3 or other people, groups, or organizations you'd like to target in the left-hand column in the table that follows. You may not have all the information you need at this point; however, take a stab at it and see what you currently know as well as what you'll need to find out.

In case you still need to be convinced that connecting with your target audiences is important, picture throwing darts without a bull's-eye to target. You point with no aim, you throw, and your dart lands anywhere. How do you know if you've succeeded if you don't know what you're targeting? If instead you aim at a bull's-eye, you'll know exactly when you've hit the mark.

Take it from Steve Orr, MarketWatch Radio Network anchor: "People pitch us stories, and it drives me crazy when they have no idea what we do. I'll ask them: 'Do you realize we're a business radio network?' There's nothing worse than a PR person's calling us with a story that has nothing to do with what we cover."

Targeting your audiences is not as much an exact science as it is considering an aggregate of many variables, including their needs, moods, cultural background, financial status, personal chemistry,

What You Can Offer Your Target Audiences

Your Target Audience (Write the names of individuals, groups, or organizations in the lines below.)	What Problem You Can Help Them Solve (i.e., Their WIIFM)	Why You're Qualified to Help Them	The Best Time to Reach Them	The Best Way to Reach Them (e.g., E-mail, Text Message, Phone, Letter, through a Mutual Acquaintance)	Who You Know in Common (i.e., for a Possible Introduction)	How Often You Can Reach Them (e.g., Daily Blog, Monthly Newsletter, Holiday Card)

Life after the White House

"I was walking my dog, Charlie, and I passed a restaurant with the doors open so I could see inside," says author-actor Laurie Graff. "There was a man sitting front and center, facing the outside. I said, 'Oh, my God, that's Bill Clinton." She continues: "My book (*Looking for Mr. Goodfrog*) had come out two weeks earlier with a little section in it about Bill. I flew with Charlie back to my apartment, screaming to my mother on my cell phone, 'I'm going to give Clinton a book!' We both love him. I grabbed one of my books, ran back to the restaurant, asked a busboy to watch Charlie, and said to a waiter while pointing at Clinton: 'I just need to give him something. I'll be a second.' Clinton looked up with those beautiful blue eyes, and I said, 'Excuse me, I don't mean to interrupt, but I wrote this book and it just came out and I want you to have it and you're in it.' I went to walk away when he said, 'It's a funny thing, because I happen to love frogs. I collect them. Not real ones. Figurines. I have about 200 at home.' Then we got to talking. I told him how much I missed him as president. I said I thought Chelsea would like this book. Clinton said he would read it. Six months later I sent him a copy of my prior book (*You Have to Kiss a Lot of Frogs*) with a letter thanking him for his kindness the night we met. He wrote back and thanked me. He makes people feel like they count."

So, how did Graff target her audience? She took a risk, seized the moment, and offered a gift—a book she had just written that has glowing references to Clinton. She could have assumed that Clinton, given his high profile and how much he's been written about, wouldn't be interested. Instead, she took a chance, risked rejection, and just went for it. She emanated confidence in her book and showed genuine warmth and enthusiasm toward Clinton.

How did Graff promote herself? If Clinton says a good word about the book to anyone, what an endorsement! How did Clinton promote himself, in turn? He connected on a human level and lived up to his reputation of making Graff feel as if she were the only person in the room. I'm sure she didn't make that a secret to her vast network!

timing, and so much more. If that sounds overwhelming, keep in mind your advantages as an introvert. You're more inclined to learn as much as you can about your audiences and think deeply about how you can make a difference to them. "Take the pulse of the situation and listen to what your animal instincts are telling you," says Marianna Lead, Ph.D., founder of Goal Imagery® Institute. "You'll see that it's not about you, and it's not about them. Instead, it's about a new entity: *you-them*." She continues: "How intimate, truthful, and real you want this relationship to be depends on how intimate, truthful, and real you are willing to be within that moment."

Look at the line-up of people and/or organizations you've identi-fied as targets in the preceding table. What do they have in com-mon? Are they mostly single urban women in their thirties or retired suburban men in their sixties? Do most of them have advanced degrees? Are they demographically diverse, yet all tend to be highly competitive? Also consider sociological factors and other prefer-ences, such as religion, affiliations, and hobbies, that they have in common. It's okay if you don't see any patterns. However, the more you can identify what they have in common, the more you can steer your self-promotion in the right direction.

COLLABORATING WITH YOUR TARGET AUDIENCE

The owner of a consulting firm—let's call him Francis Kelly—contacted me because he needed a coach to help him prepare for a major presentation. Despite his self-confidence and career success, he was terrified of speaking to large audiences. He said he wanted to find a coach in Connecticut because he preferred not to travel to New York City, where I'm based.

When I asked Kelly to envision how a coach could best help him, he described the type of support he needed with planning and rehearsing for a major upcoming presentation. I could have given him a few names of public speaking coaches in Connecticut. However, since I felt a strong connection with him, believed that

I could help him immensely, and didn't mind the 45-minute train ride to his office in Connecticut, I told Kelly I'd like to work with him. He signed up.

My conversation with Kelly was a collaboration rather than a sales pitch. I promoted myself successfully to this prospective client by asking him to describe his goals for coaching, and together we created a game plan. I could have taken Kelly's request for a coach in Connecticut on face value, referred him to another coach, and moved on. However, by asking questions and learning more, I found a valued new client, and he found the support he needed to make an outstanding presentation—a mutual win.

So it can be useful to delve into a prospective client's needs to determine how we can best help him. How do you get beneath the surface and discover his actual needs and wants? Tap into your introverted inclinations to listen and think deeply, and then find ways to be helpful. None of this should feel as though you're pushing. The more we can get to know our prospective clients and employers on a human level and find out what matters to them, the better we are at promoting ourselves to them.

Be clear about what you can offer members of your target audiences—whether they're actual decision makers who can hire you or people who influence them. While it may also be appropriate to say what you *can't* offer, lead with the positive. Describe what you *can* do, rather than starting with the hard truths about how you can't make all their dreams come true.

GAINING MUTUAL BENEFIT

When we promote ourselves to someone successfully, the result is often that both parties benefit. In the case of Kelly and me, he got a coach to help him overcome a major stumbling block in his career and I got a new client whom I was delighted to work with. I never had to "sell" Kelly on my services. All I did was listen actively and ask open-ended questions; ultimately, we found a solution together that benefited both of us.

PROMOTING YOURSELF TO SOMEONE MORE SENIOR

Do you find it more challenging to promote yourself to someone more senior, or advanced in her career, than you? While doing so can be intimidating, keep in mind the benefits that the senior manager stands to gain from learning what you have to offer. For example, you could potentially fill a staffing need for the senior manager. You might even reinforce her networking clout when she gets to call a colleague to offer a match for his organization (e.g., you or someone in your network).

Organizations don't typically hire people as a favor. More likely they hire because they have a need to fill and they're looking for results. So articulate the results that you can offer. There's also something to be said for allowing someone to be generous toward you and then showing your appreciation. Then, when the time comes, you can find ways to be helpful in turn—by doing something the other person will value, such as sharing knowledge and making introductions.

WHY YOU HIRE PEOPLE

Businesses don't hire people. People hire people. When I reflect on my own hiring decisions, I realize that personal connection plays a big role. Gary Osland, account director at mNovakDesign, agrees: "If I have a choice between two people to do a job, my criteria are: 'First, can they actually execute?'" he says. "The next is: 'Do I trust them?' And the third, if everything is equal: 'Who do I like best?'"

When you're in a position to hire, what makes you pick one candidate over another? Why do you choose a particular dentist, hairdresser, babysitter, or staff member at work over another equally qualified one? Is trust the most important criterion when you hire an accountant and a sense of aesthetics when you choose an interior decorator? Or do you have different priorities? Think about what has influenced you to pick the people you have picked. Has it been their passion for their subject matter? Their connection to you? The level of confidence they've inspired in you? Cost? Convenience? Something else? This thinking process will help you step outside yourself and ultimately gain insight about why someone would hire you.

WHY PEOPLE HIRE YOU

Using your reasons for hiring others as a backdrop for the following exercise, now let's look at why people hire you. It's easy to make assumptions. The real answers can be elusive. So let's consider why someone would hire you or contract your services—beyond the nuts-and-bolts job requirements that so many candidates meet.

Use your introverted abilities to go inward and think deeply to begin to find your answers. Think about what you wrote in the preceding table titled What You Can Offer Your Target Audiences. How much overlap is there between what you can offer and what your target audiences have appreciated about you in the past? What do they value overall? After you've gone inward, this might be a good time to do a little market research to learn more. If it's appropriate, ask trusted bosses, clients, and even managers at places where you've done volunteer work throughout your career specifically why they've chosen to work with you. You may be surprised by their answers.

Assuming that you and the other candidates have comparable levels of experience and expertise, note in the grid that follows the top reasons you think people have hired you or contracted your services. First write the name of one of your managers or clients at the top of each column. Then write a 1 for the reason you think was most important to each target audience, 2 for the next most important one, and so on. Of course, if you do ask these stakeholders, add in the actual reasons they give you.

Reasons People Have Hired You			
Reasons	Target Audience 1 *Name:*	Target Audience 2 *Name:*	Target Audience 3 *Name:*
Trust			
Convenience			
Your fee and/or compensation level			
Your passion			
Comfort			
Confidence			
Thoroughness			
Prominence in field			
Warmth			
Family and/or friend connection			
Reliability			
Freebies you offer			
Efficiency			
Your office space			
Your office staff			
Other:			

Many of my clients have shared that their human connection with the hiring manager was pivotal in their getting the job, assuming that their qualifications were on a par with those of the other candidates. This realization has helped them focus on the importance of building relationships, rather than wasting energy trying to "sell" themselves or overemphasize their qualifications.

WHAT YOU TAKE FOR GRANTED ABOUT YOURSELF

After completing the Reasons People Have Hired You exercise—especially if you actually asked others why they hired you—you may have found that some of the main reasons your bosses and clients have had for hiring you are qualities you take for granted about yourself. These may include some of your most stellar qualities, yet you haven't noticed them because they come easily to you or they've always been there. Still, these qualities may be what others most appreciate about you.

In the space that follows, name three of your qualities that you take for granted at least some of the time. Mine are these: (1) I can often hear the subtext, or what's not being said, in a conversation. (2) I have a high level of compassion. And (3) I'm adept at creating orderly systems out of chaos. Do I remind myself of those traits every day? Well, it wouldn't kill me, especially if these are qualities my target audiences value. It's important that I'm at least aware of these qualities.

What do you take for granted about yourself? List three of your assets that you sometimes forget about in the space that follows. It might help to refer back to the responses you received when you informally surveyed your dream team regarding what they appreciate about you in Chapter 1. It might help to do a little market research here too and to get input from a confidante or two.

1. _____

_____

2. _____

_____

3. _____

_____

What insights have you had by thinking about what you take for granted about yourself? From my experience, the clearer you are about your assets, the clearer others will be. How can becoming more aware of what you take for granted about yourself help you in targeting your audiences? It's back to the definition we started with at the beginning of this chapter. To effectively target your audiences, look at the overlap between what they want and what you've got. You have a lot of attributes. Which ones do your target audiences value most?

QUALITY CONNECTIONS

Anne Houle, senior manager for leadership training at Saks Fifth Avenue, has this closing advice on the value of targeting people who seem right for you: "Quality connections, not quantity, are especially important for an introvert. Cultivate one-on-one relationships, and believe your gut as to whom you can trust."

To exemplify Houle's point, one of my target audiences is made up of introverts who hire me to coach them on their self-promotion efforts. These clients have all made a commitment to work on something essential to them and have entrusted me as their thinking partner and stalwart supporter. Whether I work with them for six weeks or a year, the relationships often become deep, and we can forever become a part of one another's professional networks. These clients are also a source of referral business. For all these reasons, I strongly value and nurture those relationships. How does this apply to you? Target people who are a good match for you, who will become welcome additions to your network, and who won't drain your energy.

Now that you've identified your target audiences and explored what they value in you, in the next chapter you'll go outward to meet them and learn how to apply more of your introvert's advantages to further boost your buzz.

REFLECTIONS AND ACTIONS

What You Learned

1. _____

_____

2. _____

_____

3. _____

_____

Action: What will you do?	How You'll Do It: What support or further information will you obtain?	Accountability: Whom will you tell about this action?	Completion Date: By when?

five

Your Network

Expanding Your Sphere of Influence

This story is real. Some details have been changed because . . . well, it's a small world. "It was a bloodbath," whispers a Chanel-clad HR executive whom we'll call Ginger Parker. "They canned my boss and put my nemesis in charge of the department. I called in sick the next day and made a list of everyone I could possibly contact," she says. "It was red-alert time. I had to get the hell out."

Parker, who is an introvert, shares how she got into gear: "I brainstormed names of everyone I could think of—friends, family, former bosses, clients, colleagues, people from elevators, shoe stores, Jacuzzis, and bat mitzvahs." She reflects: "Thankfully, over the years, I had always been generous about connecting people, sharing information, leads, staying in touch, and offering my talents as a problem solver.

"I didn't realize how many people would be happy to help me," Parker continues. "The outpouring of support was phenomenal and landed me my next job within a few months in an unexpected way. An acquaintance I had met bungee jumping in New Zealand a year earlier offered to introduce me to a colleague. The acquaintance was a bond trader. I was a senior human resources manager—different worlds—but within a few weeks, I got a sizzling hot offer at a competitor, and packed my bags and never looked back."

Parker's story demonstrates the value of networking, which we'll define as building business relationships for mutual benefit. Networking works best as a lifelong pursuit rather than as self-promotion CPR when you need a job or want to power up your business during down times. "I treasure that I have a lot of people in my network and that I can help make connections," says Gary Osland, account director at mNovakDesign. "No matter what my colleagues are looking for—whether it's a good speech writer, chiropractor, or a locksmith—they come to me. I value that they put trust in my recommendations." He adds: "And the goodwill usually comes back to me."

> The world would be a much better place if everybody knew one great stunt, magic trick, or practical joke to pull on their friends.
>
> **—Mac King, comedy magician, Las Vegas**

As an introvert, you'd probably rather listen than talk most of the time. You're adept at building deep and lasting relationships. You're trusted, accountable, and a core contributor. People look to you for your expertise. However, you're not a schmoozer. You value your space and quiet time. Regardless, you have distinct advantages that enable you to create a strong network that can provide you with continuous support.

Why network? A CareerXroads study of name-brand firms' use of networking found that the number 1 external source of new hires was referrals (28 percent), while the second largest source was online job boards (26 percent).[1] So from the standpoint of hiring organizations, word of mouth is the best way to find you. Likewise, if you're an independent consultant or business owner, your network—including the clients and colleagues who sing your praises—is probably what pays your bills. So how are prospective clients and employers going to find you unless you tell people in your network that you're for hire?

In this chapter we'll talk about how you can apply your existing gifts and resources to strengthening your professional network. However, before you make your first phone call, identify what you can offer, who will be interested, what's in it for the other party, and what you want from your network. We'll cover getting recognition for your expertise; intercultural aspects of self-promotion; the ways you spend your networking time; and your sphere of influence—that is, who you know; how to ask for help; how to have informational interviews, which can help you expand and deepen your network; and how to break the ice in social situations. We'll also discuss your elevator pitch, or the all-important answer to: "So tell me about yourself"; how to handle business cards; and how to present yourself with confidence. All you need to get started is a computer, a phone, and a smile. Ready?

POSITION YOURSELF AS A VALUED EXPERT

Shoya Zichy, author (with Ann Bidou) of *Career Match*, offers you advice that will help you raise your visibility: "Join organizations, volunteer your time, and take on special initiatives within your company." She adds: "Find projects in which you can work with people from other departments, and be generous with your expertise. Also, write for company and industry publications whenever possible." Zichy emphasizes the benefit of this approach for introverts: "Rather than being known for your charm, you become known as an expert providing a valuable service."

Zichy gives the example of the former CEO of a Fortune 500 company she knows who is deeply introverted. Her contact was aware that he needed additional visibility, but he just wasn't the type to schmooze in clubs in the Hamptons. Instead, as an art expert, he joined the board of a major museum. "That's a big reason why all these people serve on volunteer boards," says Zichy. "It's often because of who will be sitting next to them." Volunteering on a board will allow you to interact regularly, possibly over the course of a year or more, with others who share a common interest with you. This will give you ample opportunities to form deep, lasting relationships with a select few of your fellow volunteer board members. Perfect for an introvert.

Getting Guidance

We have an organization at Baruch College called Executives on Campus, which brings executives and working professional people to the campus to mentor, coach, and guide the students. It enables the students to network with peers across industries. I can't tell you how many people have made career changes or job changes through the connections they made at EOC.

—Kathleen Waldron, Ph.D., president of Baruch College

NETWORKING IN THE SPIRIT OF SHARING

You can reframe self-promotion as a more palatable activity by approaching it as a way of connecting and sharing with people you would enjoy knowing. One of my clients went out of his way to help three of his colleagues this week. He didn't ask for anything in exchange—and he didn't need to. A gifted but unassuming introvert, my client helped his colleagues because he enjoys connecting talented people with attractive opportunities. The generosity usually comes back to him, often in spades, and often when he's least expecting it. He doesn't push or pressure anyone. Of course, not everyone subscribes to the spirit of sharing. However, my client surrounds himself with people who understand the value of relationships and who look out for their colleagues over time.

So you're a lawyer who addresses the needs of someone who has been wronged and is entitled to justice. You're a technical writer who can translate complex concepts into plain English. Conveying these gifts is not just self-promotion—it's letting others know that you have what they need. Kathleen Waldron, Ph.D., president of Baruch College, suggests a forum to help you spread the word: "You by fatigue, constipation, and digestive disorders. Sulfa drugs can deplete PABA by destroying the beneficial bacteria in the bowel that produce it. If taken together with folic acid, PABA increases estrogen levels.

Adult RDI: None given.

Best sources: Liver; brewer's yeast; wheat germ; molasses; and green, leafy vegetables.

Vitamin C

This vitamin is soluble in water and easily destroyed by exposure to air. Vitamin C is an antioxidant, assists healing, and fights infection. It helps in metabolizing protein and is important in making collagen—the substance underlying skin, tendons, ligaments, cartilage, and blood vessels. Collagen is used to repair tissue. Vitamin C works with iron to build the blood, helps make the neurotransmitter norepinephrine, and has a slight antihistamine effect. Large amounts of vitamin C are found in the adrenal glands. Vitamin C is depleted rapidly under stressful conditions. High intake of vitamin C will not reduce stress but will help reduce the free radicals created by stress-induced body chemistry changes.

Vitamin C deficiency is signaled by poor digestion, bleeding gums, easy bruising, anemia, low resistance to infection, poor lactation in new mothers, and shortness of breath. Chronic deficiency results in scurvy, which can be fatal if not treated. Standard treatment for scurvy is taking vitamin C–rich foods.

Adult RDI: 60 milligrams.

Best sources: Acerola; citrus; tropical fruits (mangoes, guavas, papayas); all fruits; and green, leafy vegetables. A single guava may have 240 milligrams of vitamin C. Juiced acerola berries provide 4 grams of vitamin C in an 8-ounce glass (in comparison, an 8-ounce glass of grapefruit juice has 93 milligrams and the same size glass of orange juice has 124 milligrams).

Bioflavonoids

Bioflavonoids are not vitamins, but they accompany vitamin C in natural plant sources and are thought by many nutritionists to be necessary for adequate absorption and effectiveness of vitamin C in the body. They are water-soluble and are made up of rutin, citrin, hesperidine, flavones, and flavonals. They are in the white, soft pulp surrounding citrus fruit on the inside of the peeling and are found in many other fruits, vegetables, and herbs.

Antioxidant activity has been demonstrated by bioflavonoids, which are believed to assist vitamin C in keeping collagen in good condition. They strengthen blood vessel walls. Bioflavonoids are natural anti-inflammatory agents. Rutin is used to alleviate varicose veins and to reduce hemorrhoids. Bioflavonoids are found in the same foods as vitamin C.

FAT-SOLUBLE VITAMINS

Vitamins A, D, E, and K make up the fat-soluble vitamins. They are circulated in the blood and delivered to tissues dissolved in lipids, and any of the fat-soluble vitamins in excess of body needs are stored in body fat. Because storage allows large amounts of these vitamins to be stockpiled in the body, toxicity is a very real risk. Vitamins E and K are not toxic in large quantities, but vitamins A and D can be very toxic. I am not including carotene (provitamin A) as a fat-soluble vitamin, although it can be converted into one.

Our bodies can store up to a year's supply of vitamin A and, beyond that, additional intakes become very dangerous. Ten times the normal 5,000 IU RDI is toxic for most adults, but five times normal intake is dangerous if consumed for several months. Damage due to vitamin A toxicity affects the same organs involved in deficiency symptoms —the eyes, skin, salivary glands, kidneys, bones, joints, and immune system. Nausea, cramps, pain, vomiting, diarrhea, menses disrupted, skin sores, weight loss, pain in calves, and intense bone pain are both symptoms and consequences of excess intake of vitamin A.

The current RDI for vitamin D is 400 IU. That is based on a "worst-case scenario" in which an otherwise healthy person has no exposure to sunlight. (People who are exposed to sunlight three times a week for fifteen to twenty minutes get enough vitamin D.) There is no extra benefit from taking more than 400 IU daily. Excess vitamin D causes calcium to be dissolved from the bones and deposited in muscle tissue, blood vessel walls, and internal organs. In the kidneys, it forms kidney stones. Other symptoms and effects are loss of appetite, frequent urination, vomiting, diarrhea, fatigue, muscular weakness, dizziness, confusion, high blood pressure, kidney failure, and coma.

The fact that vitamins A, D, E, and K are fat-soluble vitamins emphasizes our need for a sufficient intake of fats and lipids so that these vitamins can be delivered to the tissues that need them. That is not usually a problem for Americans, who consume far more fat in the diet than people of most other nations, but it could be a problem for people trying to maintain a low-fat or a no-fat diet. Balance is a key principle in all aspects of diet and health.

Vitamin A

Provitamin A in the form of beta-carotene is what we encounter in yellow fruits and green or yellow vegetables, and it is this substance that is transformed into vitamin A by enzymes. Scientists tell us that provitamin A is anticarcinogenic. Vitamin A is important to vision, growth, bone-building, the reproductive system, nerve sheaths, and the health of mucous membranes. It helps nourish skin, teeth, and gums. Deficiency is marked by night blindness, increased frequency of colds and catarrhal conditions, weight loss or failure to gain weight (in children), and loss of fertility.

Adult RDI: 5,000 IU.

Best sources: Cod liver oil; carrots; broccoli; tomatoes; milk; cheese; butter; eggs; meat; asparagus; apricots; muskmelon; cantaloupe; papayas; peaches; prunes; watermelon; and all green, leafy vegetables.

Vitamin D

This vitamin, like vitamins A and E, is a fat-soluble vitamin. Nicknamed "the sunshine vitamin," vitamin D can be formed by the action of ultraviolet light from sunlight acting on a close relative of cholesterol in the blood capillaries just under the skin. With all the cholesterol in the average American diet, you would think most people would have plenty of vitamin D, but apparently that isn't the case. There would be a great plague of rickets if artificial vitamin D were not being added to milk, yet I can't help feeling that people would be better off with the natural vitamin D, if they could get it.

Vitamin D deficiency in children causes inadequate assimilation of calcium from the bowel and causes trapping of phosphorus in the kidneys. As a result, bones don't grow right, which results in bowed legs, knock-knees, enlarged wrists and ankles, spinal curvature, softness of the skull, and irritable nervous behavior. In children, the disease is called rickets; in adults, it is called osteomalacia. Adding vitamin D to the diet solves the problem and cures the disease.

In adults, vitamin D helps maintain the nervous system, regulates blood-clotting capability, and keeps the heartbeat stable. It strengthens the teeth throughout life. The largest supply of vitamin D in the body is stored in the liver, but it is also found in the skin, spleen, and brain.

Deficiency signs may include frequent respiratory infections, restlessness, and constipation. The RDI for vitamin D is 400 IU daily for those who spend most of their time indoors. Excess vitamin D can cause nausea, vomiting, diarrhea, weariness, and calcification of soft tissues, which may lead to kidney failure.

Most nutrition researchers list only animal products as sources for vitamin D, and the only vegetarian source I have been able to find is a yeast source. Fish liver oils are common sources for vitamins A and D, which work well together. In combination, they may reduce the number of colds. Most people are able to synthesize the vitamin D they need by getting a little sunlight every day.

Adult RDI: 400 IU.

Best sources: Fish liver oil, eggs, butter, fatty fish, and vitamin D–fortified milk. There's an effective synthetic vitamin D available in health food stores for strict vegetarians.

Vitamin E

Vitamin E is not a single substance but a group of fat-soluble compounds called tocopherols, related chemically to alcohol. Heat will not break down vitamin E, but exposure to air will. Because vitamin E takes up oxygen slowly, it is able to protect fatty acids, other vitamins (like vitamins A and B), and enzymes from oxidation. This antioxidant helps prevent the formation of free radicals like peroxides, which increase cancer risk and accelerate the symptoms of aging. The role of vitamin E in human sexuality is not well researched but is assumed on the basis of animal experiments. Vitamin E is believed to assist in muscle function and is known to protect the liver from damage. Whether it helps relieve symptoms of heart disease isn't known, but it does prevent clots from forming. It promotes energy production and cellular respiration. It protects pituitary and adrenal hormones and may increase oxygen assimilation by the brain.

Very little is known about deficiency symptoms of vitamin E because deficiency (at least identifiable deficiency) in normal people is unknown. Many people take 400 IU because of this vitamin's many benefits.

Adult RDI: 30 IU.

Best sources: Cold-pressed vegetable oils, raw seeds, raw nuts (especially almonds and hazelnuts), wheat germ oil, beans, vegetables, liver, mango, sprouts, and kale.

Vitamin K

Vitamin K was discovered in Denmark and is found in alfalfa and other green vegetables, especially the leafy vegetables. It is abundant in wheat grass and barley grass, as well as being manufactured by beneficial bacteria in the bowel. Antibiotics can cause vitamin K deficiency. When chemically isolated, vitamin K compounds are yellow oils that are not harmed by heat or air but are destroyed by ultraviolet light. Cooking doesn't disturb it.

Vitamin K has two main jobs in the body. One is to help make the substance prothrombin, the blood-clotting factor, in the liver. The second is to promote bone formation.

Vitamin K is not known to cause any problems when taken in excess, but the artificial, water-dissolved forms of vitamin K are toxic. Excess may cause damage to red blood cells and/or stimulate the liver to release bile pigment (which can damage the brain).

Adult RDI: 80 micrograms.

Best sources: Green, leafy vegetables; blackstrap molasses; eggs; milk; yogurt; safflower oil; and fish liver oils.

CHEMICAL COMPOSITION OF THE HUMAN BODY

The forty-one chemical elements that make up our bodies exist naturally in soil, water, and foods in various molecular combinations as well as electrically charged atoms called ions. We group these molecular combinations and single elements into convenient categories like amino acids, fatty acids, electrolytes, trace elements, and others. Some of these elements exist in our bodies only in molecular combinations, while others may operate either individually or in combination with other elements. In the early 1900s, a German food chemist named Georg Augustus Koenig, who taught at Harvard University, measured the amounts of different elements in the human body (see Table 6.1).

Table 6.1. **Koenig's Composition of the Human Body**

Element	Percentage	Element	Percentage
Oxygen	72.00	Chlorine	0.09
Carbon	13.50	Fluorine	0.08
Hydrogen	9.10	Potassium	0.026
Nitrogen	2.50	Magnesium	0.012
Calcium	1.30	Iron	0.01
Phosphorus	1.15	Iodine	trace
Sulfur	0.15	Silicon	trace
Sodium	0.10		

Since Professor Koenig's day, researchers have come up with a far more complete picture of the elements that make up the human body. Now we know there are twenty-one chemical elements essential to human life, including the carbon, hydrogen, oxygen, and nitrogen that make up water, protein, fats, and carbohydrates but not much else. There are a handful of other elements that may have health benefits but are not considered essential. These include nickel, vanadium, arsenic, tin, silicon, boron, and strontium. (Germanium may have health benefits but is not normally found in the human body.) That leaves thirteen elements found in bone, fat, and some internal organs for which there is no known function. These include rubidium, aluminum, lead, cadmium, barium, gold, zirconium, cesium, mercury, beryllium, uranium, and radium. The heavy metals lead, mercury, cadmium, and beryllium are toxic when found above certain levels in the body. (Nearly *all* metals are toxic at some level of intake.)

The total number of nutritional substances critical for human life was finally established in the 1970s in the development of total parenteral nutrition (TPN). In 1970, a young Canadian woman named Judy Taylor underwent surgery for massive internal gangrene that required removal of her small intestine. Since the small intestine is where protein, fats, and carbohydrates are broken down and taken in through the intestinal wall and where vitamins, minerals, and trace elements are also assimilated, there was serious concern about how to keep her alive.

The answer was total parenteral nutrition. The term *parenteral* means "bypassing the normal digestive organs," usually by intravenous feeding of liquid nutrients. A leading expert in parenteral feeding, Dr. K. N. Jeejeebhoy, was called in from Toronto to take responsibility for keeping Ms. Taylor alive. He succeeded, despite a number of difficult problems that had to be overcome, such as how to mix lipids and fat-soluble vitamins with water-soluble nutrients. The process was fine-tuned in the ensuing years, but now we know which nutrients are necessary and which are not. That is not to suggest that scientists will not find other nutrients and chemical elements that *improve* health and well-being. But they have discovered all the essential nutrients necessary to sustain a reasonable quality of life.

Considering that carbon, oxygen, hydrogen, and nitrogen are predominantly found in protein (muscle, connective tissue, membranes, hormones, hemoglobin, and so on), carbohydrates, fats, and water, we have about 97 percent of the body weight in those chemical elements. I will not be discussing these in the following section because they are nearly always in molecular form in the body. They don't "behave" as individual elements when linked together in molecules; they function in the particular manner of their combined form. That leaves 3 percent in bone elements, electrolytes, trace elements, and some miscellaneous nonessential elements that just happen to be in the body (mainly stored in the bones and fat). We will now go over the categories of chemical elements used in the human body.

MAIN BONE-FORMING ELEMENTS

To be entirely accurate, there are lots more chemical elements that make up our skeletal structure than calcium, magnesium, and phosphorus. Beside that, the "big three" bone-makers are also important electrolytes (or parts of electrolytes) that we'll be discussing in the next group of elements. Finally, the actual bone matrix is made of protein, mostly collagen, on which calcium phosphate, calcium carbonate, magnesium salts, and other minerals are deposited. Bones are about half water and half solids. Our bones are like "coat hangers" that we keep the rest of our bodies on, so they are very important.

Calcium

Calcium is one of the most important elements in the body, forming bones by working together with phosphorus, magnesium, copper, manganese, zinc, boron, fluoride, sodium, strontium, vitamins A, C, and D, and traces of other chemical elements. Ninety-nine percent of the calcium in the body is used for bones and teeth, and the other 1 percent is shared by many body functions. Calcium is not well assimilated from foods, and exercise is very important in making sure assimilated calcium is used and not eliminated by the kidneys.

In the last two decades, the apparent epidemic of osteoporosis in postmenopausal women has been a wake-up call to the fact that most Americans don't get enough calcium. In the late 1800s and early 1900s, rickets and osteomalacia, respectively, were epidemic in cities—evidence of calcium deficiency in children and adults (usually caused by vitamin D deficiency). The average intake of calcium these days is about 640 milligrams, according to studies by the National Institutes of Health (NIH).

The National Research Council has set the required amount of calcium at 1,000 milligrams daily for healthy adults and children four or more years old. Recent studies by the NIH indicate that 1,000 milligrams daily may not be sufficient to meet the needs of long-term, chronically calcium-deficient people. It is safe to take up to 2,500 milligrams of calcium if you are in good health.

Calcium is one of our primary electrolyte elements, the other three being magnesium, potassium, and sodium, essential to cellular metabolism. Calcium is required for blood to clot, nerve transmission, muscle stimulation, stabilization of the acid/alkaline (pH) level of the blood, and maintaining water balance. It is important in enzyme reactions, blood pressure, and may help prevent colon cancer. The bones are also used as a storage repository for calcium and other minerals. Hormones act as chemical messengers, either to send excess blood calcium to be stored on bones or to signal the bones to release calcium into the blood. Calcium works with magnesium to help regulate the heartbeat.

Adult RDI: 1,000 milligrams.

Best sources: Milk products (including all cheeses), oysters, tofu, kale, broccoli, mustard greens, parsley, watercress, asparagus, cabbage, kelp, raw nuts and seeds, whole cereal grains, legumes, soy powder, yeast, carob, figs, and prunes. Broccoli is the best vegetable source, but it would take 4½ pounds of it to meet the RDI. It would take over 3 cups of raw almonds, 6 cups of raw, hulled sesame seeds, or 230 prunes to meet the RDI for calcium. Still, every little bit counts. Drinking a quart of milk or eating a quarter pound of cheese per day would bring in close to 1,000 milligrams of calcium. Lactose-intolerant persons can now purchase lactose-free milk at most supermarkets and get the calcium they need. Most Americans who don't use dairy products probably don't get enough calcium, although orange juice and other drinks are being fortified with calcium carbonate these days. The problem is that calcium carbonate interferes with iron absorption. The best calcium supplements to use are calcium citrate, calcium gluconate, and calcium lactate, and they should always be taken at mealtime together with magnesium and vitamin D.

Phosphorus

Phosphorus, another of the great bone-building elements needed by the body, is important in cell reproduction, conversion of carbohydrates to energy, and stabilizing the acid/alkaline balance of the blood. Adults have 1½ pounds of it in the body, of which 80 percent is used for bones and teeth. It is seldom deficient because it is present in most of the foods we eat—which is good news because phosphorus is needed by every cell of the body.

Like calcium, phosphorus has many tasks in the body. Adenosine triphosphate is created in cells to generate energy. In the form of phosphatidylcholine in lecithin, it makes up (together with cholesterol) the protective nerve sheaths that form the white matter of the brain, the coating of the spinal cord, and the nerves that run for hundreds of miles through the body.

In lecithin, it helps keep cholesterol and fats in solution in the blood and helps transport fatty acids. Many enzymes and most B vitamins work only in the presence of phosphorus. This element takes part in the processing of all three major food groups—proteins, carbohydrates, and fats. It is essential to cell division through its role in nucleoproteins and is necessary for kidney functioning. As part of the phosphate ion PO_4, it forms an electrolyte that helps in the passage of nutrients into cells and wastes out of cells. At least 70 percent of the phosphate in foods is absorbed, but if sugar is present, the calcium-phosphorus relationship is disrupted. Phosphorus is needed for healthy nerves and a healthy heart.

Adult RDI: 1,000 milligrams.

Best sources: Meat, poultry, fish, dairy products, nuts, seeds, legumes, vegetables, and fruits.

Magnesium

Magnesium, like phosphorus, is available in so many foods that most of us get plenty of it in food—and that's good, because magnesium is an important element in the body. About 60 percent of the magnesium in our bodies is found in the bones and teeth with calcium and phosphorus, so magnesium qualifies as one of the top three bone-builders. Something like 40 percent of magnesium is used in body fluids as a multipurpose element, doing everything from spark-plugging enzymes to helping the heart muscle relax on the downside of the heartbeat. It is an important and busy electrolyte, helping control what goes in and comes out through cell walls, converting fats, protein, and sugar to energy, boosting nerve signals along nerve pathways, and helping control the pH of blood and body liquids. Even though there is plenty of magnesium in food, researchers have found some evidence that a deficiency of magnesium may set off heart attacks. The problem is, the amount of magnesium that remains in the body depends on how much calcium there is. Previously, I pointed out that the average American gets around 640 milligrams of calcium per day, 360 milligrams short of what is needed. Since calcium intake limits the amount of magnesium the body can accept, inadequate calcium intake can cause a shortage of magnesium in the body, even if magnesium is abundant in the foods you eat. It is possible that inadequate magnesium favors kidney stone formation. Experiments have shown that small supplements of magnesium helped prevent kidney stone formation by driving out the calcium that normally helped form the stones.

Adult RDI: 400 milligrams.

Best sources: Rice bran; millet; leafy, green vegetables; legumes; and soybeans are rich sources of magnesium. Nuts and seeds are fair sources, while nearly all other natural foods have at least small amounts of magnesium. Many processed foods have no magnesium content. The last three chemical elements discussed are not only important as bone-builders, but along with the next three, they are valuable as electrolytes.

ELECTROLYTES FOR LIFE

Electrolytes are a fascinating subject all by themselves, but here we will skim over them without going into great detail about them. Minerals (as dry solids at moderate temperatures) are represented by chemical formulas like $CaCl_2$ because the Ca—

calcium in this case—and the Cl_2—two chlorides in this case—are bonded together electrically. (The term *chloride* is the electrically charged active form of the electrically neutral element chlorine. The same goes for the elements iodine and fluorine. Their electrically active forms are iodide and fluoride.) In water, however, the two chemical elements that make up this mineral may separate into what are called *ions*. An ion is defined as an atom that has lost one or more of its electrons and has a net positive charge or an atom that has gained one or more electrons and has a net negative charge. For convenience, positively charged ions are called *cations* and negatively charged ions are called *anions*. When the atoms of calcium and chloride in $CaCl_2$ separate in water, they are represented in chemistry shorthand as $Ca^{++} + 2Cl^-$. Now you are looking at a mineral transformed into two electrolytes.

Every cell in the body has fluid inside and fluid outside of it, with electrolytes inside the cell membrane and electrolytes in the outside fluid. These electrolytes coordinate to transfer nutrients into the cell and to collect wastes from inside the cell to expel from the body. The highest concentration of electrolytes inside the cell consists of potassium, magnesium, and phosphate, while the highest concentration outside the cell is made up of sodium, chloride, and carbonate. When the electrolyte concentration on the inside of the cell is greater than the concentration outside the cell, water flows inside the cell until the two concentrations are equal, and vice versa when the electrolyte concentration is higher outside the cell. The pressure that develops from this difference in electrolyte concentrations is called *osmotic pressure*. Obviously, cells shrink when water flows out of them and swell up when water flows into them. This process, on a scale involving the whole body, is connected with processes like cellular respiration (and energy production), blood pressure, edema, pH balance, and selective elimination (or conservation) of certain electrolytes in the urine. All these processes are vitally connected with your current state of health. My hope is that this explanation will help you see how important it is to make sure your body has all the electrolytes it needs and all the water it needs. (Dehydration due to chronic inadequate liquid intake can be devastating to a person's health.)

Sodium

Sodium, potassium, and chloride are three of the most important electrolytes in the body. (Calcium, magnesium, phosphate, sulfate, and bicarbonate are also electrolytes.) Sodium is probably the most active of the electrolytes, even helping calcium deposit on the bones. Actually, most of us are borderline deficient in what I call bio-organic food sodium, but many people, particularly men, use up to 30 grams of table salt daily on their foods and in their drinks. There are people who salt their melons and tomatoes, and who dip their celery or radishes into a little pile of salt they hold cupped in one hand. Most nutritionists consider 15 to 30 grams an extremely high-risk salt intake. It is high risk, in their view, in the sense that too much table salt is believed to contribute to hypertension. When sodium is too high in the body, it is normally excreted in the urine, along with a much larger amount of potassium. That can be very hard on the heart, which always needs an adequate supply of potassium. Personally, I believe 5 grams of table salt is an extreme, high-risk salt intake. I want to tell you why I believe that.

Table salt doesn't occur in nature. It has to be refined and purified at high heat into crystals of sodium chloride. Using it results in undesirable side effects. Taking too much creates thirst, then holds water in the body. Using more than 5 grams of table salt daily puts a person more at risk for hypertension. In other words, it acts more like a drug than a food.

In contrast, sodium in foods is surrounded by a complex of vitamins and minerals that work synergistically in a way I believe differs from the activity of sodium in table salt. In my view, we should cut out or radically limit table salt and increase our intake of food sodium. Excess sodium chloride in the diet causes excretion of large amounts of potassium in the urine, encourages calcium deposits in the joints and on the vertebrae, and attracts and holds water in the body. None of that is good news. We all need to trust natural foods more and processed foods less.

I want you to understand that there are wonderfully complex reactions in the body (of which most of us are entirely oblivious) that play a large part in how we live and move and exist as conscious human beings. Electrolytes, including sodium, are involved in critical life processes including nerve transmission, the care and feeding of cells, stability of the acid/alkaline balance, the extension and contraction of muscles, and many others. Food-derived sodium, in my opinion, helps keep calcium in solution, preventing spurs, unwanted deposits, and inflammation of joints.

Adult RDI: 2.4 grams.

Best sources: Food-derived sodium is plentiful in Capra Mineral Whey, olives, seafood, kelp, soy sauce, meat, and poultry. (Capra Mineral Whey can be ordered from Mt. Capra Cheese, 279 SW 9th St., Chehalis, WA 98532. I use it myself and highly recommend it.) Green olives contain the most sodium of any fruit or vegetable, but there is at least a little sodium in all fruits and vegetables. The best among them are raisins, dried apples, casaba melons, beet greens, chard, green string beans, and artichoke hearts. Not surprisingly, most of these are much higher in potassium than sodium.

Potassium

Potassium helps regulate blood pressure together with sodium. Ninety-eight percent of all potassium in body fluids is found in the intracellular fluid inside our cells, while sodium is in the fluid outside the cells. Potassium works with magnesium to regulate heart functions. It is needed for normal growth, enzyme reactions, and in the metabolism of proteins and carbohydrates. Kidney excretion of toxins is aided by potassium, which also cooperates with phosphorus to get oxygen to the brain.

There is a lot of potassium in most foods. Since the small bowel assimilates 90 percent of the potassium from foods, there is little chance of falling short of this mineral. Shortage can be produced by an excess of table salt sodium, which causes excessive elimination of potassium via the kidneys. Our body is usually very adept at balancing relationships of chemical elements with one another, unless we violate nature's laws by putting too much of the wrong thing into our bodies. Both sodium and potassium easily form chloride salts, which I will discuss next.

Adult RDI: 3.5 grams.

Chloride

Since chloride ions generally hook up with sodium and potassium to form salts, both outside the body in foods and inside the body in fluids, a shortage of either sodium or potassium could create a deficiency of chloride. That is, chloride usually enters the digestive system in foods that contain sodium or potassium.

This electrolyte helps red blood cells get rid of carbon dioxide and assists sodium and potassium in sending nerve impulses and joining with other electrolytes in sustaining the acid/alkaline balance. Chloride is needed for the production of hydrochloric acid for the stomach. The stomach enzyme pepsin is able to break down protein only in an acidic environment. That acidic environment is created by hydrochloric acid, which also kills bacteria that may accompany the food. The highest concentrations of chloride ions are found in intestinal secretions and in the cerebrospinal fluid.

Any excess of chloride is excreted via perspiration or in the urine. The same foods that are rich in sodium and potassium are rich in chloride, and no chloride deficiencies have been encountered.

Adult RDI: 3.4 grams.

Sulfur

Sulfur has no RDI, apparently because when our protein intake is adequate, we get the sulfur our bodies need. Sulfur is part of the structure of two amino acids—methionine and cystine—which are found in the hair, skin, nails, and joints. Burning hair smells like sulfur because it is partly sulfur. Thiamine (vitamin B_1) and biotin contain sulfur. Needed for the lubrication of joints, it is found in substances related to allergic inflammation. Sulfur may be needed for collagen synthesis. In the liver, sulfur stimulates bile production. Sulfur is in keratin, the tough protein in hair and nails, and in insulin, a pancreatic hormone that assists in controlling blood sugar level and in helping cells use blood sugar to produce energy.

Adult RDI: None given.

Best sources: Eggs are the best source of sulfur, but it can also be obtained from meat, fish, cheese, and milk.

ESSENTIAL TRACE ELEMENTS

Trace elements received their generic name *trace* because they are needed in the body in "micro" amounts or traces. Most of the known trace elements are understood with regard to what they do in the body. A few are not. Iron is the best known of all of them and is required in a larger amount than any others. Trace elements that play critical roles in the structure of enzymes are called *metalloenzymes*. From one to three different metal elements may function as the "spark plugs" that ignite an enzyme into action. (An enzyme is a protein molecule that acts as a catalyst for just one kind of chemical change in the body and is not, itself, changed in the process.)

Some trace elements take an active part in energy production by the burning of fuels through oxidation. Others fit into the structures of proteins, nucleic acids, and other molecular substances. Iron, of course, is best known for its placement in the hemoglobin molecule, of which there are many in each of the billions of red blood cells in our bodies. Iron in the hemoglobin of the red blood cells picks up oxygen from the air in the lungs and transports it to the cells, picking up the waste product carbon dioxide in exchange. Oxygen is then used in energy production, the critical stuff of life. Few people realize that the hemoglobin molecule is almost identical to the chlorophyll molecule, except that the latter has a magnesium element in the center rather than iron.

Iron

Iron is probably best known for its role in hemoglobin as an oxygen carrier from the lungs to the blood, but it is also in myoglobin, which transports oxygen from the hemoglobin into the tissues. Iron-deficiency anemia is the nation's number two deficiency disease, affecting over 60 percent of the people in this country. Being short of iron translates into being short of energy—tired, run-down, a little depressed, lacking get-up-and-go. Women may lose 15 to 20 milligrams of iron during menstruation, which must be replaced to get them as energized as they were before the loss.

Seventy-five percent of the body's total 4.5 grams of iron is invested in hemoglobin, and most of the rest is in myoglobin. Ferritin is a protein that stores iron in the liver, spleen, and bone marrow; and transferrin is a protein carrier of readily available iron. There is also a "minitrace" of iron in the brain, a cofactor in neurotransmitter synthesis of dopamine, serotonin, and noradrenalin. Iron-containing enzymes break down peroxides, convert food into energy, and increase the water content of cells, nearly always by interacting with oxygen carried to cells by iron-containing hemoglobin. Iron deficiency is most common in children under five and women.

Adult RDI: 18 milligrams.

Best sources: Blackstrap molasses, pumpkin seeds, liver, meat, fish, poultry, cereal grains, eggs, dried beans, and spinach.

A larger percentage of iron from meats is absorbed than from vegetable and fruit sources of iron.

Iodide

The average American intake of iodide is about 700 micrograms daily, probably due to the convenient availability of iodized salt. The risk of toxicity from overdosing is low. Russians and Swedes who took 100-milligram supplements of potassium iodide during the intense radioactive fallout of the Chernobyl nuclear reactor disaster some years ago did not suffer overdose symptoms—nor did they acquire damaged thyroids from the radioactive iodide that they couldn't avoid absorbing. Many who did not take the potassium iodide supplements assimilated radioactive iodide from the air and the food they ate, which damaged their thyroid glands and put them at high risk for thyroid cancer.

Goiter, an iodide deficiency disease manifesting as an enlarged thyroid, used to be common in the United States and many other nations, except for geographical areas near the ocean. In China 5,000 years ago, kelp and burned sponges were carried thousands of miles inland from the seashore to give to those who had goiter. People who ate seafood didn't get goiter. Lots of people who didn't or couldn't eat seafood did get goiter. In 1820, a Swiss doctor reasoned that the cause of goiter was iodide deficiency, but nothing much was done about it until this century.

Iodide, needed by the thyroid gland to produce thyroxin, was first extracted from seaweed in 1812, but it was not added to table salt in the United States until 1917. At that time, an estimated 90 percent of the population was deficient in iodide, and goiter was widespread. However, iodide deficiency is not always caused by lack of iodide in food. In diets where broccoli, cauliflower, cabbage, and their close relatives are frequently served, a natural chemical substance in them hinders the assimilation of iodide.

The only task iodide has in the body is to enter the thyroid gland and become part of the two thyroxine hormones, T3 and T4, which control basal metabolism. Basal in this context simply means normal—the metabolism that a calm, healthy person on a balanced diet would have after a good night's sleep. Metabolism takes in the activity level of all body organs and functions, and in this sense, iodide plays an extremely important part in maintaining health and well-being. Thyroid hormone circulates in the blood and reaches every cell of the body, where it is met by an enzyme containing copper and zinc and is changed into a form that influences the energy production in the cell.

Adult RDI: 150 micrograms.

Best sources: Kelp and dulse are the best food sources. Clams top the list of highest iodide-containing seafoods. Oysters, lobsters, and crabmeat are high, followed by ocean fish like salmon, tuna, halibut, red snapper, and cod. Fruits and vegetables grown near the seacoast also carry a significant amount of iodide.

Fluoride

Nearly all of us have fluoride in our bodies. Fluoride strengthens teeth, reduces cavities, and hardens bones. In many places, it is in the drinking water at a level of 1 part per million (ppm). Research by Finnish scientists reveals a drop of 50 percent in osteoporosis among women drinking water with 1 part per million of fluoride in it. The elderly are especially in need of this element, not only because of its activity in increasing bone density but also because of improved hearing, which may occur from recalcification of the bone structure of the inner ear.

Cardiovascular disease is helped by fluoride, which helps reduce hardening of the arteries. It prevents cavities in teeth not only by hardening the enamel but by reducing the acid in the mouth caused by carbohydrates, which, in turn, helps prevent the decay of tooth enamel.

Toxic effects begin at 2 to 8 parts per million of fluoride, causing mottled teeth. At higher levels, 8 to 80 parts per million, tendons and ligaments are calcified and degeneration of the liver and other organs takes place. Fatalities have been recorded at concentrations over 50 parts per million.

The fluoride in foods is calcium fluoride. The kind added to drinking water and toothpaste is sodium fluoride.

Adult RDI: 1.5 to 4 milligrams.

Best sources: Seafood, milk, cheese, meat, fruit, and vegetables (the latter two depend on the soil). Some water supplies are naturally fluoridated, and you should know the amount in parts per million; over 8 ppm will mottle teeth unless you take extra calcium. See your doctor about this.

Zinc

Zinc is like one of those "one-man bands" that I used to watch on amateur talent contests in the pioneer days of TV, in which the same man played drums, harmonica, trumpet, guitar, banjo, and other instruments. Zinc, for example, is required in over two hundred different enzymes needed in seemingly all aspects of human physiology. It helps make protein and nucleic acids (DNA and RNA); boosts healing and growth; protects the immune system; converts carbohydrates and other fuels into energy; enhances our senses of smell and taste (activates appetite); and is in insulin, the substance that regulates blood sugar. It helps detoxify alcohol, supports T-cell production in the immune system, aids in bone development, and helps maintain healthy skin.

In the body, it is found in the bones, kidneys, liver, pancreas, prostate gland, skin, hair, nails, spermatozoa, eyes, voluntary muscles, and white blood cells. Zinc may play a part in cancer prevention. There are two grams of zinc in the average body. At any given time, 20 percent of the body's total zinc is circulating in the blood.

Adult RDI: 15 milligrams.

Best sources: Meat, poultry, seafood, whole cereal grains, brewer's yeast, and pumpkin seeds.

Copper

Copper is required in the making of red blood cells, in getting iron assimilated from the small intestine, and in moving iron out of storage in the liver or muscle tissue. This element is required to transform fats and carbohydrates to energy. It plays a part in building strong bones and protecting us from heart disease. Nerve sheaths are formed with the help of a copper-containing enzyme. Copper supports the immune system and is an ingredient in superoxide dismutase (SOD), a natural antioxidant that is said to remove the dangerous free radical superoxide from the body. In that sense, it helps protect from cancer.

There are 75 to 100 milligrams of copper in the body. It helps form collagen, protects cell membranes, and assists in making the neurotransmitter noradrenalin. Copper helps synthesize phospholipids that are needed to form nerve sheaths, protects polyunsaturated fats from rancidity, converts tyrosine into the melanin that colors hair and skin, and takes part in the healing of damaged tissue. It is needed for bone formation, RNA production, and protein metabolism.

Copper and zinc often work together in the body, but they also compete in the diet or when supplements are used. When too much zinc alone is taken, copper can't be assimilated; when too much copper alone is taken, zinc is shortchanged. When both copper and zinc are deficient, hypothyroidism may result. The zinc-to-copper ratio in the body should be 10 to 1, and they should be taken together with other minerals—in multimineral tablets or capsules. If you are taking the RDI of zinc, 15 milligrams, your intake of copper in a multivitamin-mineral form should be limited to about 1.5 milligrams.

Most people are relatively careless about monitoring their copper intake, which is dangerous, considering all the functions copper fulfills. One study showed that ulcer patients were short in copper. Deficiency symptoms include weakness, respiration problems, and skin sores. If you're getting too little copper, you are also getting too little iron, because copper is needed for iron to be assimilated.

Copper can be toxic at an intake over 35 milligrams daily. Signs of overdose are headaches, dizziness, stomach pain, nausea, vomiting, and diarrhea. In extreme cases, coma and death may take place.

Adult RDI: 2 milligrams.

Best sources: Seafood; liver; meat; poultry; whole grains; nuts; green, leafy vegetables; legumes; avocados; soybeans; eggs; and cauliflower. The amount of a metallic element in food always depends on what is in the soil.

Cobalt

Humans can only take in cobalt in the form of vitamin B_{12}, which contains it. Livestock can utilize pasturage or feed with cobalt in it and transform it into B_{12}, but food containing the element cobalt other than in B_{12} is toxic to humans. The only reason we can say that cobalt is an essential trace element is because it happens to be in vitamin B_{12}, which is known to be essential. No reliable vegetable source of cobalt in vitamin B_{12} is known. (I have seen a study that reported B_{12} in food algae was not assimilated by the body. I can't say whether that is the last word on the subject. B_{12} is very high in chlorella, a nutrient-packed alga available in nearly all health food stores.)

Adult RDI: Unnecessary.

Chromium

Like iodide, chromium is a single-purpose trace element. In the 1950s, Dr. Henry Schroeder found out that although American babies were born with enough chromium, deficiencies were evident in the majority of them by the time they reached their teen years. Over 25 percent of adults showed no chromium in their blood tests for some decades. Many others showed a little chromium but below normal. Chromium deficiencies cause symptoms like diabetes, which is not surprising when you get a little background on chromium.

In nature, nearly all high-sugar plants, such as sugarcane and sugar beets, have chromium in them. Sugar refineries then process the vitamins and minerals out of the raw product until pure powdered or granulated sugar is the only thing left. Only in recent decades have scientists discovered that Mother Nature knew what she was doing by putting chromium with sugar.

One of chromium's jobs in the body is to be involved with sugar metabolism. It teams up with the B vitamin niacin and amino acids to form Glucose Tolerance Factor, which makes insulin more sensitive to blood sugar. Insulin is a hormone manufactured and released by beta cells of the islets of Langerhans in the pancreas. When blood sugar gets too high, insulin sends some to the liver for storage and directs the rest to cells. Too much sugar makes the blood so thick, it clogs kidney tubules and damages the lens of the eye, nerve sheaths, and red blood cells. Before this can happen, insulin directs some of the blood sugar to storage and the rest to cells where it is converted to energy. Glucose Tolerance Factor makes sugar control and assimilation by cells three times more effective than insulin by itself.

Chromium activates enzymes that metabolize fats and cholesterol. When enough chromium is present in the daily diet, blood levels of cholesterol may be lowered by 15 percent to nearly 42 percent. This lowers the risk of cardiovascular disease. It competes with iron in the transport of proteins and, if a steady dietary intake is assured, it may help prevent diabetes and hypoglycemia.

Deficiency symptoms include increased fatty acids and cholesterol in the blood, blood sugar disorders, and nerve irritation. People most at risk are the elderly, those who do strenuous exercises (like runners), and pregnant women.

Adult RDI: 120 micrograms.

Best sources: Brewer's yeast, calf liver, black pepper, cheese, oysters, wheat bran, whole wheat bread, rye bread, yellow cornmeal, and chile peppers.

Manganese

Doctors and nutritionists were surprised when patients on TPN, total parenteral nutrition, were receiving sufficient calcium in their liquid food supply but were not assimilating it. They discovered that just a little manganese was needed for the assimilation of calcium, so they added it to the TPN list of nutrients. They already knew that calcium assimilation required the presence of copper and zinc. Most adults have between 10 and 20 milligrams of manganese in their bodies, mostly stored in the liver, kidneys, and bones.

Manganese is needed in several important body functions. One enzyme that fights free radicals requires manganese as a coenzyme. It is needed by several enzymes that metabolize fats and cholesterol, build protein, and synthesize the nucleic acid RNA. Manganese is essential in making the neurotransmitter dopamine. Epileptics and schizophrenics are often deficient in manganese.

When manganese is lacking, low energy and fatigue are present, usually together with backaches, skin lesions, and nerve problems. Lack of sufficient manganese can lead to degeneration of bone and cartilage, including spinal disks. Deficiency of this element eventually causes heartbeat irregularity, fertility problems, dizziness, birth defects, and impaired growth. If the deficiency isn't taken care of, convulsions may result.

Adult RDI: 2 milligrams.

Best sources: Hazelnuts, chestnuts, buckwheat, turnip greens, beet greens, beets, brussels sprouts, oatmeal, millet, and cornmeal.

Molybdenum

Molybdenum deficiency is seldom encountered because it is widespread in foods. In fact, too much molybdenum intake blocks copper assimilation, which results in anemia. Long-term copper suppression results in bone demineralization. Molybdenum is essential because it is required in three enzymes—one that mobilizes iron reserves from the liver, a second enzyme that metabolizes fats, and a third that breaks down sulfites.

Adult RDI: 75 micrograms.

Best sources: Lentils; beef liver; split peas; cauliflower; wheat germ; brown rice; spinach; garlic; eggs; and green, leafy vegetables.

Selenium

Selenium and vitamin E are said to work wonderfully well as a team in destroying free radicals, protecting the heart from angina attacks, and improving circulation limited by cardiovascular disease. This same team appears to improve the quality of life for muscular dystrophy patients, to alleviate autoimmune diseases like osteoarthritis and rheumatoid arthritis, and to increase the effectiveness of the immune system.

Operating solo, selenium may lift energy levels, prevent cataracts, and relieve the pain and stiffness associated with arthritis. It binds to toxic metals, such as mercury, cadmium, silver, and thallium, and ushers them out of the body. It protects cell membranes in the liver, kidneys, heart, and lungs. Selenium is necessary for the production of prostaglandins that affect blood pressure and has an anticlotting effect that reduces the risk of stroke and heart attack. It is considered essential for reproduction. Selenium is concentrated in the liver, heart, spleen, and kidneys.

Some doctors and nutritionists are recommending intakes of 200 micrograms daily.

There is much yet to be learned about this trace element. It may help prevent numerous diseases, including cardiovascular disease, alcohol-induced cirrhosis of the liver, emphysema, arthritis, hypertension, and cancer.

Deficiency signs include premature aging, cataracts, retarded growth, liver necrosis, and, over the long term, heart disease and cancer.

Adult RDI: 70 micrograms.

Best sources: Liver, brewer's yeast, broccoli, cabbage, mushrooms, celery, seafood, onions, garlic, whole cereal grains, cucumbers, and radishes.

TRACE ELEMENTS: ESSENTIAL IN THE FUTURE?

Four trace elements—nickel, vanadium, tin, and arsenic—are being taken seriously as potentially essential for human life. Experiments have shown that animals need them. The question is, do humans? So far, TPN has kept a large number of people alive for up to thirty years or so without them. However, most people have them in their bodies, so we are going to describe what is known about each one, then move along to the next category of trace elements.

Nickel

Nickel activates several enzymes involved in hormone and fat metabolism and protects cell membranes. It activates trypsin, arginase, and carboxylase in the liver. Iron–deficiency anemia may be aggravated by nickel deficiency. When it was withheld from the feed of experimental chickens, their legs changed. The experiment was repeated with other animals, and the need for nickel-activated enzymes was again verified. The assumption is that nickel does *something* essential with its coenzymes in the human body. But TPN patients are doing fine without it. It's obviously health enhancing, but is it essential?

Best sources: Seafood, cereal grains, hydrogenated fats, buckwheat, legumes, seeds, cabbage, broccoli, and cauliflower.

Vanadium

The status of this trace element was based on experimental rats that developed hair loss, skin problems, cessation of growth, and skin lesions when vanadium was withheld from an otherwise complete diet. More recently, it has been shown that vanadium is in most body tissues and helps regulate sodium in the body. That could well qualify it as essential. It may yet be added to TPN.

Best sources: Liver, seafood, meat, vegetable oils, legumes, radishes, and dill.

Tin

Experiments with lab animals have shown that a deficiency of tin interferes with growth and with hemoglobin production. Unless enough iron and copper are around to counteract the deficiency, anemia will result. Estimated requirement is 3 to 4 milligrams daily. It is in widespread use in industry and finds its way into the human body as a contaminant, mostly from air pollution. Whether it is taken into body tissues from the lungs is unknown at this time. About 4 milligrams daily intake from food is estimated.

Arsenic

We all know arsenic is poisonous in macro-plus amounts. But when a trace amount was withheld from experimental rats, their growth stopped, their fur grew rough, and their spleens became abnormally enlarged. We all have a little arsenic in our systems. But does it do something essential? Time and further research may tell. Food sources are not listed at this time.

HELPFUL BUT NONESSENTIAL TRACE ELEMENTS

Boron

The argument for boron's inclusion suggests that it is essential for bone-building because it facilitates the absorption of calcium into the body. A U.S. Department of Agriculture experiment was set up to test boron, in which 3 milligrams were given to postmenopausal women daily. They found that subjects who took the boron lost 40 percent less calcium, 33 percent less magnesium, and a little less phosphorus than the control group when they continued taking the tablets for eight days. That is, it doesn't prevent osteoporosis, but it slows the progress of the disease to a commendable extent. It is estimated that a balanced diet will provide all the boron the body needs, from 1.5 to 3 milligrams. The experiment just referred to also resulted in a significant increase in active estrogen and testosterone in the subjects taking boron.

Best sources: Green, leafy vegetables; fruits; nuts; seeds; and whole grains.

Silicon

This bone-building element has been recognized since Professor Koenig published his data on the makeup of the human body early in the twentieth century. It is the earth's most abundant element. We have it in our bones and cartilage. Because it is concentrated most where new bone is forming, it may have an essential role in the development of bone and connective tissue. It is also believed to be necessary for the hair, nails, and skin, but TPN patients have normal hair, nails, and skin without it.

Best sources: Whole grains; oat straw tea; seafood; bell peppers; soybeans; beets; horsetail herb; and green, leafy vegetables.

Strontium

Strontium is similar to calcium in its physical properties and is found in human bones. It may stimulate bone growth and assist in the prevention of tooth decay. Research indicates that it may be involved in energy production in cells. It is nontoxic. Nevertheless, it has not been shown to be essential.

Germanium

A Japanese engineer named Asai made bold claims about the health value of germanium in the 1970s. He had developed a product he called Ge-132. The Russians picked up on his research and announced in 1989 that a synthetic germanium product blocked the reproduction of HIV in test-tube experiments. I assume that no further news about germanium from

Russia means that no further progress with Ge-132 has been made.

There is some evidence that Ge-132 stimulates the immune system. It may yet prove to block the further growth of some types of cancer. Epstein-Barr syndrome has been successfully treated with Ge-132. So far, there are no claims that germanium functions as a coenzyme or is needed to form a protein important in metabolism.

TOXIC METALS

Toxic heavy metals, such as mercury, lead, cadmium, and others, are commonly found in most human bodies due to intake from water, food, and air polluted mostly by industrial sources. They may be absorbed through the lungs, skin, and digestive system. Once in the body, they are likely to be stored in specific organs. Where do they come from? Industrial pollution, chemicals in the workplace, cigarette smoke, food additives, pesticide residues, auto emissions, food storage containers, fumes from office equipment, acid rain, paint, and natural sources.

Metal toxicity is relative. Most metals are toxic at some level of intake, but I am restricting my list here to those that are most toxic at relatively low levels. Chemical elements not essential to human life but found in most people's bodies include aluminum, beryllium, lithium, silver, cadmium, tin, antimony, tellurium, zirconium, niobium, titanium, barium, gold, mercury, lead, and bismuth. Of these, barium, zirconium, niobium, titanium, bismuth, gold, and silver are not toxic in amounts usually encountered in the environment (including foods and water). Lab tests on animals show which chemical elements shorten the life span. These include cadmium, tin, antimony, tellurium, mercury, and lead. I'm going to run quickly through my list and provide a little information about each one.

Mercury

Mercury is used in enormous amounts in industry, and for years mercury wastes were dumped into rivers, lakes, and oceans. From the water, mercury found its way into the fish, and from the fish into the people who eat fish. Air pollution is likely to contain mercury compounds from industrial use of coal. Pesticide residues on foods also contain mercury. Unfortunately, about 10 percent of the mercury ingested goes to the brain and damages nerves. Mercury poisoning in general causes genetic defects and birth abnormalities. Methyl mercury poisoning causes loss of coordination, impaired mental functioning, vision problems, and loss of hearing. Mercury is used in dental fillings, but no significant toxicity has been found. However, some dentists try to persuade their patients to let them remove the old mercury-silver amalgam and replace it with a more inert filling material.

Early signs of mercury toxicity include digestive upset, such as excessive salivation, stomatitis, and diarrhea, and neurological problems such as tremors, dizziness, moodiness, and depression. As little as 100 milligrams taken orally produces toxic symptoms. Mercuric chloride, however, is a deadly poison.

Lead

This heavy metal has been the most dangerous toxic pollution hazard of the twentieth century, mostly due to air pollution from lead in gasoline. Ingestion or inhalation of lead damages the brain and peripheral nervous system, blood-making organs, and gastrointestinal tract. Symptoms start with loss of appetite, anemia, weight loss, fatigue, and vomiting and end with seizures, coma, and death. Children are highly at risk for brain and nerve damage in exposure to lead. Leaded gas was phased out starting in the 1970s and completed in 1995, but remaining high levels of lead in urban air are due to industrial use of coal in manufacturing. Lead is deposited in the bones and other tissues.

Cadmium

The problem with the heavy metal cadmium is that it is chemically similar enough to zinc to replace it when zinc is deficient and cadmium isn't. Zinc is needed in over two hundred enzyme reactions in many different aspects of human metabolism, and when cadmium replaces zinc in these enzymes, the outcomes change and multiple dysfunctions occur. Intake of cadmium comes from cigarette smoke, food stored in zinc galvanized containers, tap water, fatty foods, cooking oils, canned foods, refined foods, coffee, tea, and alcoholic beverages. Plastic, copper, and iron water pipes all contribute cadmium to the drinking water supply. Cadmium is relatively high in soft water. Kidney breakdown is common when chronic cadmium poisoning takes place.

Symptoms of cadmium toxicity include nausea, vomiting, diarrhea, and abdominal cramps. If symptoms continue into exhaustion, dizziness, acute kidney failure, and pulmonary edema, death is likely.

Tellurium

This is a nonmetallic element that is found alongside heavy metals in ores, and it has a wide range of industrial applications. It is used in rubber and as an alloy with nonferrous metals. Exposure to this element is fairly common. A dietary source may be traced to the common can opener, which drops about 8 milligrams of filings into the food as it cuts into the metal lid. Most of us unknowingly eat these filings. Tellurium lends a pungent garlic odor to the breath.

Its toxic symptoms from higher doses include skin lesions, inability to perspire, and digestive disturbances.

Thallium

The toxicity of this element was exposed after it had been used for some years as a depilatory (hair remover). Long-term users developed chronic poison symptoms. Additionally, it is an ingredient in rat poison, which has sometimes been used to coat grain to be used as seed. Every now and then, some hungry, unknowing person uses thallium-treated grain for food, and a number of fatalities have been reported.

Symptoms of thallium poisoning are nausea, vomiting, headache, stomach pain, bloody diarrhea, elevated liver enzymes, lethargy, tremors, delirium, seizures, coma, and death.

Tin

I am including tin as a toxic trace element, even though it is also being considered as a potential essential nutrient. Rats fed 5 parts per million in water had shorter than normal life spans, but they also had liver lesions. Tin accumulates in the heart without evidence of harm, but in the intestine it may compete with copper and render copper unable to assist iron to be assimilated into the bloodstream. The only symptom that can be suggested in this case is anemia. Significant intakes of tin dissolved in slightly acidic fruit juice from "tin cans" of past years (interiors of cans are now lacquered) were not known to cause problems for humans.

Aluminum

In laboratory experiments with rats, aluminum did not shorten their average life spans, but we do know enough about its effects on the human body to include it as a toxic trace element. Antacids containing aluminum prevent the absorption of phosphorus and calcium in the small intestine. It destroys vitamins; and aluminum salts in the blood eventually cause fatty degeneration of the liver and kidneys and weaken the tissue of the gastrointestinal system.

Aluminum intake may come from foods (especially table salt and baking powder), drinking water, commercial antacids, cookware, aluminum foil, deodorants, emulsifiers added to foods, and a bleaching agent in wheat flour. It is well absorbed by the body, with highest concentrations in the brain, lungs, liver, thyroid, and arteries. Acidic foods like rhubarb cooked in aluminum pans dissolve a lot of aluminum. Daily intakes may range from 10 milligrams to over 100 milligrams, depending on a person's lifestyle, diet, tap water, medications, and environment.

Toxic symptoms of excess intake include loss of appetite, constipation, nausea, skin problems, fatigue, and excessive perspiration. The late Adelle Davis recommended taking magnesium as an antidote to excess aluminum in the body. Continuing intake of aluminum salts may result in localized numbness and motor paralysis.

Antimony

Antimony caused heart disease in rats and shortened their life spans, so it has become classed as a toxic element. There are records of people having been poisoned by antimony assimilated into food from the enamelware in which it was served. This element is found in the human body in the amount of nearly 6 milligrams. Symptoms have not been recorded.

CHAPTER 7

JUICING FOR LIFE

You need to realize that juicing is not just one of those things you should pick up and lay down when you want to. The quality and longevity of your life depend on regularly meeting your body's nutrient needs. And longevity is relatively meaningless when life degenerates into one disease, disturbance, and doctor bill after another. Longevity and a high quality of life together are precious.

One of the reasons I'm so glad to see a juice trend catching on in this country is that it may signal a move away from overeating protein, fatty foods, salty foods, and dairy products that I believe are killing us. I still hear too many men saying, "I'm a meat-and-potatoes man," although not as much as I used to hear it.

Another reason I'm favorably impressed with people who are joining the juicing movement is that I believe a genuine concern for better health is taking place, in the very face of health-care costs so high that none but the rich (or the well-insured) can financially survive a lengthy hospital stay. One way to lower health-care costs is for more people to stay healthy and keep out of hospitals and doctors' offices.

OTHER LANDS, OTHER PEOPLE

In all my travels, the places where I've found the oldest living persons—such as the Hunza Valley, the Caucasus Mountains, Turkey, Vilcabamba (Ecuador), and others—were never urban, never highly cultured, never populated by the rich and famous.

People born in high-poverty areas with rich soil and limited amounts of food don't eat sparingly simply because they want to; they do it because they have to. This is one of their secrets—they have to eat sparingly and they have to work very hard every day. Do we have to be compelled to do what's good and what's right for ourselves? It's something I'm concerned about, because conditions seem to be degenerating worldwide.

One of the old men I talked to in the Caucasus Mountains of the former USSR answered my questions through an interpreter. I asked, "What is your advice for living such a long life?" "Just keep breathing," he said. He was well over one hundred years of age, a beekeeper in his earlier years. He didn't have access to any processed foods in his lifetime, except stone-ground flour.

GOOD HEALTH MUST BE EARNED

I realize that juices and juicing are a wonderful trend, but I hope you and your friends realize that good health is not a gift from the Creator, but an opportunity to express your appreciation for the gift of life by working hard every day to sustain high-level well-being.

The true joy of life is only real joy if it can be expressed in a state of health in which the quality of life is understood and appreciated. It's hard to feel wonderful when you feel terrible, if you know what I mean. And the right way to take care of our aches and pains is to prevent them from taking hold in our lives by choosing to live the right way, by choosing to take the higher path.

Good health must be earned. Do you know of anything else more worth working for than your own good health?

I hope you continue to enjoy juicing, but I hope you will also stop and take a minute to think about your health and your life. Do you want to stay healthy as you grow older? Do you want to have the energy and motivation to live an interesting life and meet your goals with a sense of meaningful achievement?

Remember, you are juicing for life, and if you want that life to stay as nice as it is, make a commitment to enter into the kind of lifestyle that has satisfaction and happiness as two of its main side effects.

CHAPTER 8

CHILDREN AND JUICES

W̲e find that the nutrition intake of the mother-to-be is what determines the nutrition intake of the developing embryo, and the juices described in this book, taken by the mother, can assist in providing the variety of vitamins, enzymes, minerals, and other nutrients to assure the best of health to both mother and child during and after labor and delivery. I personally feel it is better to get vitamins and minerals from foods than from pills.

After the baby is delivered, mother's milk is the best food for the newborn. For the first three days of breast-feeding, a protein-rich fluid called colostrum is taken by the baby, which provides the globulins and other immune factors to protect the child from a broad variety of diseases and afflictions until his own immune system is fully functional.

During the first few months of her life, the baby's nutritional intake is obtained from the milk she drinks, and if she can't have mother's milk, she should have fresh, raw goat's milk, which is the closest to mother's milk. As long as the baby is being breast-fed, however, the mother should drink two cups of mixed carrot, celery, and parsley juices daily. If she needs more milk production for the baby, she should have more greens in juice form or in the regular diet. This will help make sure that the mother's milk includes all the nutrients the baby needs.

WHEN SHOULD INFANTS BEGIN TAKING JUICES?

Mother's milk is a whole food, able to provide all nutrients needed by the newborn, but the time comes when there is not enough of it to match the growth needs of the child. This is the time when the baby will need to take a little solid food. (I recommend that you make these at home from organically grown cereal grains, fruit, vegetables, and so forth.) There are books available to tell you how to make fresh baby food with no chemical additives. There also comes a time when juices are a timely and wise addition to an infant's early nutritional intake.

The best way, I think, to estimate when your baby is ready for his or her first juices is when the birth weight has doubled (or more) to at least 14 pounds, and the baby is breast-feeding eight to twelve times per day or taking at least 32 ounces of milk by bottle. Some doctors use other criteria, such as the age of six months, or whenever the infant is able to handle drinking from a cup with a lid and spout.

The first juices you should give your baby are apple, white grape, and pear. Juice these yourself for highest nutritional value, and make sure the pulp is strained out. Dilute half-and-half with distilled water or reverse osmosis water.

I also recommend, at this juncture in your baby's life, that you add a teaspoon of green vegetable juice to the baby's bottle of milk once every two days. The juice may be from raw spinach, broccoli, parsley, or wheat grass. Use only 1 teaspoon because the green juice is very concentrated and potent. The green juice will provide iron (in which milk is deficient), electrolytes, and chlorophyll, which will feed the beneficial bowel flora. Iron-deficiency anemia is not uncommon in infants over six months who are given lots of milk and few solids.

Juice combinations such as apple-guava, carrot-celery, apple-carrot, carrot-milk, mango-apple, pear-prune, and others can be given when your baby reaches 18 pounds. I do not encourage the use of citrus juices because they are too alkaline-forming in the stomach.

If your baby reacts to a particular juice by vomiting or diarrhea, wait another month or so and try again. If the vomiting or diarrhea reappears, talk to your doctor about it.

As the baby gets older and grows larger, gradually use less water in the juices until you are using all juice. Your baby will usually triple in weight the first year, and his height will increase by 50 percent.

When your baby has indigestion or stomach gas (burping more than usual), try a little diluted papaya juice. For diarrhea, blackberry or blueberry juice may bring relief. Dilute for babies, but use undiluted juice for infants over a year old.

I don't want to give the impression that your goal should be to give your child undiluted, pure juice as soon as possible. Not at all! Some juices will always be so strong that they should be taken diluted with some milder juice or with raw goat's milk. Green juice, whether from broccoli, spinach, kale, or wheat grass, should always be diluted 3 to 1 with a milder juice such as carrot, carrot-celery, apple, or apple-carrot. The wonderful advantage of mixing juices is that you can almost always find a combination that is pleasing (or at least acceptable) to your child.

OLDER CHILDREN CAN HELP

The way to get older boys and girls interested in juicing and juices is to invite them to help. Juicing, supervised and assisted by an adult, is an exciting challenge to children. The adult should be the one to cut fruit into juicer-acceptable chunks, unless the child is old enough, skilled enough, and responsible enough to be allowed to use a knife. When kids help, they usually want to sample the different juice combinations to find out how they taste. If you offered them some of the same juices in a glass, without their participation, many kids would say no—especially to vegetable juices. But, usually, you can find a way to make even the most bland, bitter, or sharp-tasting vegetable juice acceptable to your child by diluting it with enough apple juice to make the flavor more fruitlike. Children like fruit flavors more than they do vegetable flavors.

Apple juice or carrot juice can be mixed with almost any other fruit or vegetable juice to make it taste better.

Don't try to cram a lot of nutrition information into your five-year-old or even your fourteen-year-old child for that matter. Let them ask the questions, and they'll get further into it themselves without you doing any persuading or insisting.

One of the greatest ways of pouring in all the vitamins, minerals, enzymes, and other nutrients your child needs to stay healthy and full of life is to get her into the habit of drinking four glasses of different juices every day.

Among the most important groups of chemical elements needed by every growing child are the electrolytes, which include sodium, potassium, calcium, magnesium, chloride, phosphate, and bicarbonate. Juices, like human body fluids, are charged with electrically active chemical elements and molecules. The electrolytes play a very important part in making the human body healthy and active, and we can get these vital nutrients from juices.

JUICES, WATER, MINERALS, AND TRACE ELEMENTS

A newborn baby, after nine months in the warmth and comfort of his mother's amniotic fluid, comes into the atmosphere of earth with a body that is nearly 75 percent water. Water is the basic liquid substratum of blood, lymph, tears, saliva, intercellular fluid, intracellular fluid, cerebrospinal fluid, urine, glandular secretions, and all other body fluids. Water, next to oxygen, is the most important nutrient in the human body, and while breast-fed newborns get enough water in their mother's milk, formula-fed babies may not.

Because of the iron in formula, some babies become constipated, a symptom of dehydration. Under those circumstances, the baby should be given 2 to 4 ounces of water daily. Consult your pediatrician concerning whether your tap water is okay for the baby. If in doubt, or if you use water from your own well, boil it for ten minutes to kill any bacteria.

When babies react to cow's milk formula with allergy symptoms, goat's milk should be tried, but it must be supplemented with folic acid, which is lacking in goat's milk. A pediatrician should be consulted in these situations. Most people don't realize that dehydration can increase production of histamines, adding to the severity of allergic reactions. The baby can be given 2 ounces of water to see if symptoms abate.

Drinking water is often a significant source of minerals and trace elements needed in human nutrition, but we must not forget that water itself is a nutrient. When it is deficient, dehydration occurs, accompanied by fatigue, listlessness, and frequently constipation. If you ask most pediatricians what would happen if your infant was not drinking enough water, they would probably tell you that it can't happen, that children drink when they are thirsty. Most of the time, they do. Thirst normally appears after the body loses 1 percent of its water. However, not all infants' thirst centers are equally sensitive to the body's need for water. For roughly the first six months of life, a baby's need for water is satisfied by mother's milk or a healthy formula substitute.

Fruit juice may first be offered when the infant is drinking from a cup, usually in the latter half of the first year. Juice should be fresh and should be limited to 4 ounces. If parents give their infants too much juice too soon, appetite can be decreased for other needed nutrients. The three most important elements in the first year of a child's life are calcium, iron, and zinc—calcium for bone growth, iron for blood building, and zinc for growth. If a child develops chronic diarrhea and is not doing well, always consider the beverages she is drinking, including the amount of juices, and talk this over with your pediatrician.

At four to six months, iron-fortified infant cereals are introduced. Moisten the cereals as necessary with mother's milk, water, or a little rice milk. With your blender, you can make your own rice, barley, oat, and soy cereals, and add a little green juice for iron. Iron deficiency is most common in children from six months to three years old, a time when adequate nutrition is extremely important. Most infants double in weight the first half of the year and triple the second six months. They need all the right nutrients to allow them to grow to their fullest potential, physically and mentally.

To protect your child's teeth from unnecessary caries, avoid giving him drinks, snacks, or foods containing sugar except at mealtimes and perhaps two or three snacktimes. Sucrose is the primary villain in caries. Brush the child's teeth after every meal and introduce the idea of rinsing the mouth out after every sweet drink. Obviously, freshly made fruit and vegetable juices are much superior to commercial products like sodas, fruit punches, and Gatorade and its taste-alike competitors, but don't deprive your child completely of such drinks or you will breed resentment and rebellion. Start early teaching your child good health habits.

The following guidelines in Table 8.1 will help you understand your child's need for specific nutrients.

As your infant grows into the toddler stage, he will be able to receive, enjoy, and profit from natural, fresh fruit and vegetable juices and juice combinations. Of course, you know that it is important to start a child with simple juices like apple or pear, sometimes diluted with water. One-half cup of grape juice contains 10 IU of vitamin A, 0.2 gram of vitamin C, 0.035 milligram of vitamin B_1, 0.045 milligram of vitamin B_2, 0.08 milligram of B_6, no B_{12}, 0.35 milligram of niacin, 0.05 milligram of pantothenic acid, 3.5 micrograms of folic acid, 11 milligrams of calcium, 0.035 milligram of copper, 0.3 milligram of iron, 4.5 milligrams of magnesium, and 13.5 milligrams of phosphorus. This is an example of what you can expect from juices.

Teach your children to rinse out their mouths with water after drinking juices, as well as sucrose-containing soft drinks, to protect their teeth.

Table 8.1. **U.S. Recommended Daily Allowances for Children**

Nutrient Type	Units	Infants	Under 4 Years	Over 4 Years
Vitamin A	IU	1,500	2,500	5,000
Vitamin D	IU	400	400	400
Vitamin E	IU	5	10	30
Vitamin C	mg	35	40	60
Folic acid	mg	0.1	0.2	0.4
Thiamine	mg	0.5	0.7	1.5
Riboflavin	mg	0.6	0.8	1.7
Niacin	mg	8	9	20
Vitamin B_6	mg	0.4	0.7	2.0
Vitamin B_{12}	mcg	2	3	6
Biotin	mg	0.05	0.15	0.30
Pantothenic acid	mg	3	5	10
Calcium	g	0.6	0.8	1.0
Phosphorus	g	0.5	0.8	1.0
Iodine	mcg	45	70	150
Iron	mg	15	10	18
Magnesium	mg	70	200	400
Copper	mg	0.6	1.0	2.0
Zinc	mg	5	8	15

Note: IU = international units; mg = milligrams; mcg = micrograms; g = grams.

GREAT FOOD SOURCES FOR VITAMINS, MINERALS, AND TRACE ELEMENTS

Vitamins

Most fresh fruits and vegetables are loaded with vitamins excepting vitamins D and B_{12}. You may have to add a little cod liver oil to the fresh juice to get vitamin D. You can get vitamin B_{12} from chlorella, either in tablets or granular form; blend a small amount in a little water and add to your child's fresh juice.

Calcium, Magnesium, Phosphorus, and Iron

Use mixed juices: three parts carrot juice with one part kale, broccoli, or spinach juice and a teaspoon of wheat grass juice. Citrus juices and prune juice are high in calcium.

Sodium, Potassium, and Chloride

Juice green vegetables, okra, celery, tomatoes, and sun-ripened fruits.

Zinc, Manganese, Copper, and Selenium

Most vegetables and fruits have a little of each of the first three elements; a few have selenium. Organ meats, such as liver, are rich in selenium, as are lobster and shrimp. All meat, poultry, and fish are good sources of selenium, along with some nuts such as Brazil nuts. Selenium is found in small amounts in some fruits and vegetables. I believe that some soils in our country may be deficient or very low in selenium, and in such soils you can't expect fruits and vegetables to take in that cancer-fighting antioxidant element.

∾ CAUTION

Medical professionals caution against giving babies honey or Karo syrup in any form their first year. It can cause serious harm.

REMINDER: JUICES ARE FOODS

We have to keep in mind that juices are foods, despite the fact we use them as a supplementary backup to fill in the nutrients we may not have received from our regular diet. And the problem is not diet alone. Many people who eat right do not have the best digestion or assimilation of nutrients. This is an area where juices help pick up the slack.

Nutrients from juices are easily digested and assimilated quickly, flooding all the constitutionally weak organs, glands, and tissues with the vital nutrients needed to prevent deficiencies and support a healthy lifestyle.

You owe it to your children's future health and well-being to teach them about juices and juicing. Get them started now.

PART 2

BLENDING NATURALLY FOR HEALTH AND WELLNESS

CHAPTER 9

THE ABCs OF BLENDING

Unlike juicers, which separate the liquid of the fruit or vegetable from the pulp, blenders liquefy the pulp and juice together. Blenders are especially good for creating combinations—juices with solids, different fruits or vegetables, fruits with seeds or nuts, and so forth. Liquefied foods and combinations are not digested and assimilated as fast or as well as juices, but they are taken up faster than a meal of solid foods. And they provide fiber for the bowel.

The main advantage of liquefied foods is that you can combine foods that have the specific nutrient combinations you want, which may not be available in a single vegetable or fruit.

Selecting and buying a blender that will meet your needs takes the same kind of thought and research as buying a juicer. I suggest that you go to the library and read the consumer magazines or books on blenders to get an idea of relative prices and performances, then go to several health food stores and talk to the clerks about the kind of blender that would be best for you.

BLENDER DRINK BASES

For fruit drinks, choose your liquid base from the fruit juices, as they add flavor and value: apple, grape, pineapple (unsweetened), blackberry, elderberry, pomegranate, mulberry, wild cherry, blueberry, or raspberry.

For vegetable drinks, try to choose a vegetable base: carrot, celery, mixed greens, or tomato juice. Liquid chlorophyll (usually from alfalfa), available at your local health food store, can be used as a base or added to the base. Add 1 teaspoon chlorophyll to 1 cup water. Whey (powdered) can also be added: 1 tablespoon to 1 cup water.

Herb teas with or without leaves or seeds, such as fenugreek or alfalfa, can be a base for either fruit or vegetable blends. Select according to preference or for any particular medicinal need, for example, papaya for beneficial effect on kidneys and digestion of proteins, comfrey for general healing and for the bowel, huckleberry for starch digestion.

Vegetable broth seasoning, 1 teaspoon to about 1 cup water, makes an excellent protein drink base.

For both fruit and vegetable drinks, you can use goat's milk as a base, as well as rice milk, soy milk, and coconut, seed, and nut milks.

Drinking raw vegetable cocktails is one of the best ways of supplying needed minerals to the body. They should not be used in place of raw vegetable salads but rather to supplement them. Drink them at any time of the day or with any meal. Any water left over after steaming vegetables should be used in vegetable cocktail bases, never discarded. The presence of solid particles makes vegetable juices conducive to chewing. These blender drinks are concentrated foods and not to be taken as a "drink." *They should be chewed to mix the food with the saliva.*

SWEETENERS

Soaked raisins, dates, figs, or sweet prunes are wonderful for improving taste; black walnuts soaked in water, apple juice, or pineapple juice are very good to cover a "nasty" taste. Unsulfured molasses can be added as a healthful sweetener in beverages. (It contains B complex vitamins.) You can also use date sugar, maple syrup, or carob powder.

PROTEIN DRINKS

Make protein drinks by adding cottage cheese, egg yolk, nut butters, and milks, preground nuts and seeds, soy powder, protein or amino-acid powders, and other prepared supplements.

CARBOHYDRATE DRINKS

Add barley or other whole grains, cooked or soaked. Baked potato with the skin is a good way to use up leftovers—mix with one or two root vegetables; leeks; green, leafy vegetables; parsley; herbs; and seasoning.

For an especially nutritious drink, have one of the raw nut or seed milk drinks, or blend nut or seed milk half-and-half with carrot juice. Add a banana to nut or seed milk for a delicious smoothie.

VEGETABLE DRINKS

VEGETABLE COCKTAIL

2 cups tomato juice

1 small stalk celery with leaves,
   chopped

2 to 3 sprigs parsley

2 slices lemon

1 slice green pepper

1 slice onion

¼ teaspoon vegetable broth
   seasoning (optional)

½ teaspoon honey

Blend all ingredients until liquefied. Makes 3 to 4 servings.

BEET BORSCHT DRINK

⅓ cup carrot juice

⅓ cup beet juice

¼ cup cucumber juice

1 tablespoon lemon juice

Blend all ingredients and serve with spoonful of yogurt on top.
Makes 1 serving.

CARROT JUICE COCKTAIL

1 cup carrot juice

¼ cup any green juice and/or

1 to 2 green leaves (outer leaves
   of endive or romaine are good)

2 sprigs parsley

½ teaspoon vegetable broth
   seasoning or any desired herb
   for flavoring

Blend all ingredients. Makes 1 serving.

GARDEN-FRESH TOMATO JUICE

2 medium-sized or 1 large
   ripe tomato, sliced

Vegetable broth seasoning
   to taste
Pinch of favorite herb

Blend tomatoes without adding any other liquid. A little vegetable broth seasoning may be added, and a pinch of your

favorite herb. Once well blended, strain through a fine sieve and chill. Makes 1 serving.

WATERCRESS COCKTAIL

2 cups pineapple juice
    (unsweetened)
1 bunch watercress
3 tablespoons honey or raw sugar

1 thick slice lemon or
2 tablespoons lemon juice
1 cup cracked ice

Blend until watercress is liquefied. Makes 2 servings.

BORSCHT-YOGURT DRINK

1 cup yogurt (reserve
    1 tablespoon for topping)
½ small lemon, peeled, seeded
½ cup diced beets

½ cup diced carrot
¼ diced cucumber
1 teaspoon vegetable broth
    seasoning

Blend all ingredients until velvety smooth. If desired, pulp may be strained through sieve. Top with spoonful of yogurt. Makes 2 servings.

CARROT-PARSLEY COCKTAIL

⅔ cup carrot juice   6 sprigs parsley (well rinsed)

Blend ingredients. Makes 1 serving.

CARROT-SUNFLOWER MILK WHIRL

¾ cup sunflower seeds   3 cups carrot juice

Blend sunflower seeds until finely ground. Add previously made carrot juice; blend for a few seconds. For extra nourishment, add 1 tablespoon of lecithin liquid when blending. Makes 4 servings.

FRUIT DRINK SUGGESTIONS

MELON COCKTAIL

Liquefy the whole melon, seeds, rind, and pulp, for a delicious, highly nutritious cocktail. Melon is better used apart from meals, but occasionally include fresh apricots, prunes, apple, peaches, or pineapple for variety.

WHOLE WATERMELON DRINK

Take desired quantity of watermelon and cut into cubes, including fruit, seeds, and rind. Just a little water in the blender will start it off, and the cubes of the whole melon can be piled loosely to fill container three-quarters full. Blend smooth. Repeat until all cubes have been blended. Strain the drink through coarse wire strainer to catch seed hull fragments.

BLENDED FRUIT DRINK

1 tablespoon fruit concentrate   *1 cup pineapple juice, milk,*
(cherry, apple, or grape)   *nut milk, coconut milk, or*
                                                     rice milk

Combine as desired. Other fruits that can be added are bananas, blueberries, strawberries, plums, peaches, apricots, blackberries, and raspberries. Makes 1 serving.

TAHINI PINEAPPLE DRINK

½ cup hulled sesame seeds or   *A few drops lemon juice*
sesame butter
2 cups chilled pineapple juice

Put sesame seeds in blender and blend until very fine; blend longer to make a butter. Add pineapple juice and lemon juice and blend again. Good as a bedtime sleep coaxer. Makes 3 servings.

PINEAPPLE OR ORANGE YOGURT SUPREME

1½ cups yogurt   ½ cup orange or pineapple juice
  2 tablespoons honey

Blend all ingredients until smooth. This is a very wholesome drink, and if desired, you can add 1 tablespoon of lecithin liquid or soy lecithin granules or 1 teaspoon rice polishings. Makes 3 to 4 servings.

FRUIT COCKTAIL DRINK

8 ounces pineapple juice   4 ounces black cherry juice
1 tablespoon coconut   1 teaspoon honey
¼ cup black walnuts   ½ cup tofu
1 banana

Blend all ingredients. Makes 3 to 4 servings.

CARROT-PINEAPPLE SUPREME

½ cup cubed carrots   ½ cup cubed celery
1½ glasses chilled pineapple juice   1 tablespoon lecithin granules

Blend all ingredients until smooth. Makes 2 servings.

APPLE-PECAN FRUIT DRINK

1 apple with skin, diced   1 banana, peeled and quartered
6 pecans   8 ounces pineapple juice
3 teaspoons raisins

Blend all ingredients until well blended. Makes 2 servings.

ORANGE-STRAWBERRY DELIGHT

1 cup fresh or frozen
   strawberries (partially thawed)
1 cup orange juice
1 cup ice cream or 1 cup cracked ice

2 tablespoons honey
1 tablespoon lecithin
   granules

Blend all ingredients until smooth. Garnish with a strawberry
or a piece of orange. Makes 3 to 4 servings.

PINEAPPLE SUNFLOWER WHIRL

½ cup sunflower seeds
1 banana, peeled and quartered
A few drops lemon juice

2 cups pineapple juice
1 tablespoon lecithin granules

Blend sunflower seeds until finely ground. Add remaining
ingredients and blend until smooth. Any fruit juice can be used
in place of pineapple juice. Makes 3 to 4 servings.

PINEAPPLE-GRAPE CHILLER

3 cups chilled grape juice,
   unsweetened
2 cups chilled pineapple juice,
   unsweetened

1 cup orange juice
2 thin slices lemon rind
2 tablespoons lecithin liquid

Blend all ingredients until smooth. Makes 7 to 8 servings.

ALFA-MINT ICED TEA

1 cup water
1-inch piece lemon peel
1 lemon, peeled and quartered
1 tablespoon honey

1½ quarts hot alfa-mint tea
   (made as directed on package)
4 to 5 sprigs fresh mint
   (optional)

Put water, lemon peel, lemon, and honey in blender and blend well. Add prepared alfa-mint tea and mint. Let stand 25 minutes and strain. Chill until ready to serve. Honey may be used when serving, if desired. Makes 8 to 10 servings.

FRESH MINT FREEZE

½ cup honey	*1 tablespoon chlorophyll*
1 cup water	*(for color)*
1 cup fresh mint leaves	*1 cup whipped cream*
½ cup lemon juice	

Heat honey and water (don't boil) until honey is well dissolved. Add mint leaves and blend until leaves are finely ground. Cover and let stand until cool. Stir in lemon juice and add chlorophyll. Strain into ice tray, discarding mint pulp, and freeze until mushy. Turn into chilled bowl and beat with electric or hand beater until smooth. Fold in whipped cream and freeze until firm. Makes about 3 servings.

QUICKIE BREAKFAST IN A GLASS

1 tablespoon flaxseed meal	*1 teaspoon honey*
1 tablespoon sesame seeds	*½ cup any fresh fruit*
1 tablespoon lecithin granules	*1 tablespoon wheat germ flakes*
1 cup skim whole milk	*2 to 3 drops lemon juice*
1 egg yolk, raw	*(optional)*

Blend flaxseeds, sesame seeds, and lecithin granules until finely ground. Add remaining ingredients and blend until smooth. (This should be chewed as a food to mix with the saliva.) Makes 1 serving.

"AHEAD OF TIME" LUNCH DRINK

2 tablespoons sunflower seeds, sesame seeds, or almond nuts

1 cup apple juice

½ cup chilled, unsweetened pineapple juice

½ cup orange juice

1 raw egg yolk

1 teaspoon raisins

1 sprig parsley or watercress

2 spinach leaves

1 celery stick cut into 1-inch pieces

½ carrot, cut into small pieces

2 tablespoons wheat germ

1 teaspoon rice polishings

1 tablespoon lecithin granules

1 cup iced water

Blend seeds or nuts until finely ground. Add remaining ingredients and blend until smooth. Makes 3 to 4 servings.

MINT-LIME DRINK

1 cup boiling water

2 tablespoons honey

1 cup fresh mint leaves

1 quart chilled water

¼ cup lemon juice

1 cup lime juice

Ice cubes (optional)

Blend boiling water, honey, and mint leaves until finely ground. Chill. Strain into large container, then add chilled water, lemon juice, and lime juice. Stir until well mixed. Add an ice cube to each glass, if desired. Makes 6 to 7 servings.

POMEGRANATE JUICE AND GOAT WHEY

2 large or 3 small pomegranates

2 cups liquid whey

Extract pomegranate juice in juicer. Add to whey and serve immediately. Makes about 3 servings.

FRUIT PUNCHES

LEMON-MINT PUNCH

6 sprigs fresh mint

2 cups water

1 cup honey

2 cups lemon juice

Pinch of sea salt

1 quart unsweetened
grape juice

Mix mint, water, and honey in a pan. Simmer 5 minutes and strain. Add lemon juice and salt. Place in refrigerator until cold. Mix gently with grape juice and serve chilled. Makes about 16 to 18 servings.

PINEAPPLE-BEET "PICK-ME-UP"

2 cups unsweetened pineapple
juice, chilled

1 cup raw beets, diced

1 tablespoon lecithin liquid
or granules

Blend all ingredients thoroughly. If desired, add other ingredients such as wheat germ or rice polishings. Makes 3 servings.

PINEAPPLE-CARROT DELIGHT

2 cups pineapple juice, chilled

1 orange, peeled and quartered

1 tablespoon lecithin granules
or liquid

1 medium carrot, sliced

1 tablespoon honey

Chipped or cubed ice (optional)

Blend all ingredients until very smooth. Serve well chilled. Add chipped or cubed ice when serving, if desired. Makes 3 to 4 servings.

MILK DRINKS AND FROSTED SMOOTHIES

Soy Milk and Soy Cream

Soy milk powder is available in every health food store. For soy milk, add 2 tablespoons of soy milk powder to 1 pint of water. Sweeten with raw sugar, honey, or molasses and add a pinch of vegetable broth seasoning. For flavor, you can add any kind of carob powder or fruit.

Keep in the refrigerator. Use this milk in any recipe as you would regular cow's milk. It closely resembles the taste and composition of cow's milk and will sour just as quickly, so it should not be made too far ahead of time. Soy milk may also be substituted for rice or goat's milk in recipes.

BANANA MILK

1 cup goat's milk
½ cup any fruit juice

1 ripe banana
1 tablespoon honey

Blend all ingredients until smooth. Makes 1 serving.

DATE MILK DRINK

5 pitted dates
1 cup goat's milk

1 teaspoon powdered coconut
1 teaspoon nuts

Blend all ingredients until creamy. Makes 1 serving.

CARROT MILK

1 cup goat's milk

1 medium-sized carrot, chopped

Blend all ingredients until very fine and smooth. Makes 1 serving.

BANANA FIG MILK SHAKE

½ cup soy milk
½ cup fig juice
1 teaspoon rice polishings

1 banana, very ripe
Carob to flavor, if desired

Blend all ingredients until thick and creamy. Makes 1 serving.

CARROT-BANANA MILK SHAKE

½ cup goat's milk
1 banana, very ripe

½ cup carrot juice
1 teaspoon sunflower seeds

Blend until smooth and creamy. Makes 2 to 3 servings.

CHILLY APRICOT WHIRL

2 cups cold goat's milk
¾ cup revived apricots

1 tablespoon honey

Blend all ingredients. Chill and serve. Top with apricot half. Makes 3 servings.

"HONEY-OF-A-BANANA" MILK SHAKE

1 cup cold goat's milk
1 banana, quartered
1 tablespoon lecithin liquid

1 tablespoon honey
1 cup chipped ice

Blend all ingredients until very smooth. Makes 3 servings.

PINEAPPLE-MINT FIZZ

1 cup unsweetened pineapple
   chunks or 1 cup unsweetened
   pineapple juice

2 cups cold soy milk
1 sprig fresh mint
1 tablespoon lecithin liquid

Blend all ingredients until smooth. Makes 3 to 4 servings.

VANILLA–CHERRY SUPREME

2 cups red cherries or
  Bing cherries (reserve
  8 cherries for garnish)

2 pints ice cream
1 quart soy milk, chilled

Blend cherries, 1 pint ice cream, and soy milk until creamy. Serve in tall glasses and top each with ¼ cup extra ice cream and a cherry. Makes 8 servings.

STRAWBERRY MILK SHAKE SUPREME

3 cups soy milk, chilled
2 tablespoons honey
3 cups fresh or frozen
  strawberries, partially thawed

1 tablespoon lecithin liquid
1 pint strawberry ice cream

Blend soy milk, honey, strawberries, and lecithin thoroughly. Serve in glasses and top with ice cream. Makes 7 to 8 servings.

PINEAPPLE DELIGHT

1 quart pineapple juice,
  unsweetened

4 large ripe bananas

Blend ingredients well. Makes 7 to 8 servings.

CHERRY WHIP

2 cups pineapple juice
1 cup tart cherries or
  Bing cherries

1 slice lemon or lime
1 tablespoon lecithin granules

Blend all ingredients until smooth. Makes 3 to 4 servings.

REDUCER'S SPECIAL

2 cups pineapple juice,
   unsweetened and chilled

1 bunch watercress
1 cup crushed ice

Blend all ingredients well. Makes 2 servings.

SUNSET ORANGE GLOW

1 cup soy milk, chilled
1 orange, peeled and quartered
1 tablespoon honey

½ cup orange juice
1 lemon, peeled and quartered
1 cup crushed ice

Blend all ingredients until smooth. Makes 2 to 3 servings.

RASPBERRY DELIGHT

1½ cups chilled pineapple juice
   1 cup fresh or frozen raspberries
   2 tablespoons lemon juice

1 tablespoon honey
2 cups chipped ice
1 tablespoon lecithin liquid

Blend pineapple juice and raspberries on high. Strain to remove seeds. Return to blender and add lemon juice, honey, ice, and lecithin. Blend until smooth. This drink is delightfully refreshing and healthful. Makes 3 to 4 servings.

"GOODNIGHT" SNACK

1 cup milk
1 tablespoon lecithin granules

1 tablespoon molasses

Blend all ingredients, then warm to comfortable drinking temperature. This helps with sleeping problems. Makes 1 serving.

GOLDEN DAYBREAK MILK SHAKE

2 tablespoons sunflower seeds
2 to 3 cups goat's milk

2 tablespoons honey
3 to 4 medium carrots, cut into
    1-inch pieces

Blend sunflower seeds until finely ground. Add remaining ingredients and blend until smooth. This is a very nourishing drink for children and convalescents and can be served at any time during the day. Makes 4 servings.

APRICOT SMOOTHIE

1 cup fresh stewed apricots
1 cup goat's milk or soy, rice,
    nut, or seed milk

1 cup cracked ice
Honey to taste

Blend all ingredients until smooth and creamy. Most other fruits can be used similarly for smoothies; even vegetables such as carrot, tomato, and spinach can be used. Sesame or other nut milks may be used also. Use honey, maple syrup, or molasses if sweetening is necessary. Makes 2 servings.

COCONUT MILK DRINKS

COCONUT JUICE OR MILK

1 cup unsweetened shredded
    coconut or fresh coconut, diced
    and ground in blender

3 cups hot water

Blend half the quantity of ingredients at a time if too full. Chill. This is a delightful addition to any milk or milk drink, including soy milk. Makes 3 to 4 servings.

CARROT-COCONUT MILK

½ cup hot water

1 tablespoon fresh, grated
coconut

½ cup fresh carrot juice

Blend water and coconut. Add carrot juice. Makes 1 serving.

PRUNE MILK

¼ cup pitted prunes

Few drops pure vanilla or a
sprinkle of cinnamon

1 cup coconut milk or sesame
milk

Blend until very fine and smooth. Makes 1 serving

MOCK-CHOC MILK

1 heaped tablespoon soy
milk powder

1 tablespoon honey

½ tablespoon carob powder

1 cup water

Blend all ingredients until smooth and creamy. Makes 1
serving.

ICED MINT MOCK-CHOC

3 tablespoons carob sauce

½ tablespoon honey

¼ teaspoon vegetable broth
seasoning

¼ teaspoon pure vanilla

½ cup water

2 cups thick soy milk

1 tablespoon whey powder

4 to 5 sprigs fresh mint

1 cup cracked ice

Blend all ingredients until creamy. Makes 3 to 4 servings.

MOCK-CHOC BANANA SHAKE

2 cups soy, rice, or nut milk   ¼ cup carob

1 banana, sliced   1 dash vegetable broth seasoning

1 raw egg yolk

Blend all ingredients until smooth and creamy. Makes 2 to 3 servings.

MOCK-CHOC SESAME MILK

¼ cup carob powder   Sesame milk

⅓ cup raw sugar   Vanilla to taste

½ cup water

Combine carob powder, sugar, and water in a pan and simmer 5 minutes, stirring occasionally. Add a good tablespoon of this mixture to each cup of sesame milk. Add a few drops of pure vanilla. Blend to a frothy drink.

THERMOS DRINKS

VITAL BROTH

1 teaspoon vegetable broth   1 cup hot water
   seasoning   ¼ cup watercress

¼ cup parsley   Other greens to suit

Blend all ingredients until very smooth. Pour into preheated thermos. Makes 1 serving.

HEALTH DRINK

1 teaspoon vegetable broth   1 cup hot water
   seasoning   ¼ teaspoon dulse

1 tablespoon whey powder   Cream to taste

Blend all ingredients for a really delicious drink. Pour into pre-heated thermos. Makes 1 serving.

LUNCH IN A THERMOS

1 cup apple or pineapple juice

½ cup orange juice

2 spinach or romaine leaves

½ cup fresh fruit

1 small piece banana

½ cup carrots, diced

1 teaspoon rice polishings

2 sprigs parsley

1 teaspoon raisins

¾ cup cashews or almonds

1 small celery stalk, diced

1 raw egg yolk

2 teaspoons wheat germ

1 cup crushed ice

Blend all ingredients for 3 minutes. Add crushed ice and pour into thermos. This makes a complete meal. Makes 1 serving.

PROTEIN-CARBO DRINKS

SLIMJIM

1 cup buttermilk

1 teaspoon brewer's yeast

*1 teaspoon vegetable broth
   seasoning*

1 egg yolk

2 tablespoons wheat germ

1 tablespoon gelatin

Few drops lemon juice

Blend all ingredients. Drink immediately. Makes 1 serving.

MIAMI

1 cup papaya tea

4 tablespoons cottage cheese

3 tablespoons sunflower seeds

4 dates

Blend all ingredients. Chill and serve. Makes 1 serving.

ZEST

1 cup goat's milk	2 tablespoons skim milk powder
1 teaspoon rice polishings	¼ teaspoon dulse
1 tablespoon black walnut butter	⅓ teaspoon molasses

Blend all ingredients. Serve warm. Makes 1 serving.

HOT MOCK-CHOC

2 tablespoons carob powder	¾ cup hot nut milk
2 tablespoons skim milk powder	

Blend all ingredients and serve. Makes 1 serving.

SPECIAL PROTEIN-CARBO COCKTAIL

1 tablespoon flaxseed	1 tablespoon lecithin granules
1 cup cold goat's milk	1 tablespoon rice polishings
½ cup cheddar cheese, diced	1 tablespoon wheat germ
1 egg yolk	

Put flaxseed in blender and blend finely. Add remaining ingredients and blend until smooth. This makes a delicious-tasting and nourishing protein snack. Makes 2 to 3 servings. Dr. Jensen believes raw goat's milk is an exceptionally good protein base.

BLENDED DRINKS

These drinks are very tasty and nutritious. Try serving them to your drop-in guests.

CHERRY BONANZA

1 cup black cherry juice	2 tablespoons honey
2 cups unsweetened pineapple juice	1 banana
	1 egg yolk

2 tablespoons soy powder   1 teaspoon rice polishings

1 tablespoon wheat germ

Blend all ingredients. Makes 3 to 4 servings.

TROPIYUM BREEZE

1 banana   2 tablespoons soy powder

½ cup chopped parsley   1 cup papaya juice

2 tablespoons honey

Blend all ingredients. Makes 1 serving.

MAUI BREAKTIME

1 cup blackberry juice   1 banana

⅔ cup pineapple   ⅓ cup crushed pineapple

1 egg yolk   2 tablespoons soy powder

1 tablespoon honey   Shredded coconut for garnish

Blend all ingredients and serve with shredded coconut. Makes 3 servings.

OTHER DRINKS

EARTHDRINK

1 cup soy milk   4 tablespoons cooked cereal

¼ teaspoon dulse   (brown rice, oatmeal,

Honey to taste   or millet)

Few drops vanilla or lemon

Blend all ingredients. If cooked cereal is cold, heat with soy milk until warm. Makes 1 serving.

VEGGIE PICKUP

1 cup carrot juice   ½ cup corn (off cob)
1 stalk of celery   Vegetable broth seasoning

After blending, this can be sieved. Add a little sweet raw cream. *Note:* Sweet potatoes or yams also make a very good carbohydrate base for drinks. Makes 1 serving.

LIMA BEAN DRINK

3 tablespoons vegetable broth   1 cup cooked lima beans
    seasoning   1 tablespoon whey powder
1 tablespoon brewer's yeast   2 tablespoons cream
1 tablespoon honey

Blend vegetable broth seasoning, brewer's yeast, honey, lima beans, and whey powder until smooth. Add cream and blend a few seconds longer. Vary amount of honey to taste. Serve warm or cold. Makes 3 servings.

NUT AND SEED DRINKS

A good blender will chop seeds and nuts in three to five seconds, grind them to a powder in a little more time, or reduce them to a butter. Quick switches to "on" and "off" at high speed and a rubber scraper to scrape off the sides help. The longer you blend, the finer the butter.

By blending a liquid with your butters, you can whip up nutritious milk-substitute drinks in no time. Blended nuts and seeds can be easily digested.

Almond Nut Milk

Use blanched or unblanched almonds (or other nuts). Soak overnight in pineapple juice, apple juice, or honey water. This softens the nut meats. Then put 3 ounces of soaked nuts into 5 ounces of water and blend for 2 to 3 minutes. Flavor with honey or strawberry juice, carob flour, dates, or bananas. Any of the vegetable juices are also good with nut milks.

Nut milks can also be used as a flavoring with soups and vegetarian roasts or over cereals. Almond milk makes a very alkaline drink, high in protein, and easy to assimilate and absorb.

Seeds and Sprouts

Seeds and sprouts are going to be the foods of the future. I have been told that many of the seeds have the hormone values of male and female glands. Seeds carry the life force for many years, as long as they are enclosed by the hull. Seeds found in Egyptian tombs known to be thousands of years old have grown when planted. To get finely ground seeds into our bodies in the form of a drink gives us the best nutrition.

Flaxseed and sunflower seeds, sesame seeds, apricot kernels, dry melon seeds, and others grind dry in the blender very well. Since these seed powders deteriorate quickly, keep your blender handy and grind them as often as needed. Don't store the dry ground seeds or they will go rancid. Hulled nuts and seeds and their powders must be refrigerated to prevent rancidity.

Cantaloupe Seed Drink

Instead of throwing away the seeds and pulp from the inside of the cantaloupe, blend these thoroughly with a little pineapple juice or oat straw tea sweetened with honey; strain to remove the seed hull, and serve as a delicious nut milk drink, rich in vital elements.

Variation: Squash seeds may be similarly treated in a suitable liquid, flavored with honey or maple syrup and a few dates or sliced fresh fruit.

Sesame Seed Milk

I believe that sesame seed milk is one of our best drinks. It is a wonderful drink for gaining weight and for lubricating the intestinal tract. Its nutritional value is beyond compare, as it is high in protein and minerals. This is the seed that is used so much as a basic food in east India, Turkey, and the Mideastern countries.

Blend 2 cups water, ¼ cup sesame seeds, and 2 tablespoons soy milk powder until smooth. If hulled sesame seeds were used, strain through a fine-wire strainer or three or four layers of cheesecloth. This removes the hull fragments. (Hull-less sesame seeds can be used.)

Variation: Add 1 tablespoon carob powder and 6 to 8 dates, pits removed. For flavor and added nutritional value, blend in any of the following: banana, date powder, stewed raisins, or grape sugar. After any addition, blend well. This drink can also be made from soy, rice, or goat's milk in place of the water.

Other uses for sesame seed milk. Add to fruits, after-school snacks, vegetable broth, or cereals for breakfast, or mix with any nut butter. It can also be used as a salad dressing base. Take twice daily with bananas to gain weight, add to whey drinks to adjust intestinal sluggishness, and use with supplements such as flaxseed or rice polishings.

Sunflower Seed Milk

The same principle used for making nut milks can be employed to make sunflower seed milk; that is, soaking overnight, blending, and flavoring with fruits and juices. (Add the remaining juice used to soak the seeds to the water in the blender.) It is best to use whole raw sunflower seeds and blend them yourself. If you do not have a blender, sunflower seed meal can be used.

NUT CREAM

1¼ cups soaked seeds or nuts	2 tablespoons sesame oil
1 cup pure water	Vegetable broth seasoning
2 tablespoons honey	(optional)

Blend soaked seeds or nuts and water. Add honey, sesame oil, and vegetable broth seasoning and blend well. Makes 1 serving.

NUT MILK

For nut milk, add more water to nut cream recipe. For 1 serving, combine ⅓ cup nuts or seeds (previously soaked in apple or pineapple juice for at least 10 hours) with 2 cups (1 pint) of water or goat's milk and remaining ingredients. Refrigerate. This keeps several days.

MAPLE NUT FRUIT NECTAR

1 teaspoon pure maple syrup	3 tablespoons raw nuts
1 cup fruit juice	

Blend all ingredients. Makes 1 serving.

MAPLE NUT BANANA CREAM

1 tablespoon maple syrup

1 cup goat's, rice, soy, or any nut
or seed milk

1 tablespoon sweet raw cream

2 tablespoons chopped English
walnuts, pecans, or black
walnuts

1 ripe banana, sliced

Blend all ingredients until creamy. Serve cold or warm. Makes
1 serving.

JUMBO FRUIT/NUT DRINK

1 cup pineapple juice

½ cup black cherry juice

2 tablespoons soy milk powder

1 tablespoon coconut

6 pitted dates

1 tablespoon honey

¼ cup black walnuts

1 egg yolk

1 sliced banana

Blend all ingredients. Makes 3 to 4 servings.

SESAME-BANANA MILK SHAKE

1 cup sesame milk

3 to 4 dates, chopped and pitted

1 sliced banana

Blend all ingredients. Makes 1 serving.

SESAME FRUIT SHAKE

1 cup sesame seed milk

2 to 3 dates, chopped
and pitted

½ banana, chopped

Small slice papaya

Blend all ingredients. Makes 1 serving.

SESAME SUPPLEMENT CREAM

1 cup sesame seed milk

1 teaspoon flaxseed meal

3 to 4 dates, raisins, figs, or
  papaya, chopped

1 teaspoon rice polishings

1 tablespoon sunflower
  seed meal

1 tablespoon wheat
  germ

Blend all ingredients well and use on breakfast cereal or over fruit. Makes 1 serving.

SESAME NUT CREAM

1 cup sesame seed milk or

  1 teaspoon sesame seed
  butter in 1 cup water or
  fruit juice

½ cup nut butter

6 dates, pitted and chopped

Blend all ingredients well and serve over breakfast fruit or use as a sweet dressing for salads. Makes 1 serving.

SESAME SEED DRESSING

1 cup sesame seed meal

1 cup boiling water

1 cup cold-pressed oil

4 tablespoons vegetable broth
  seasoning

Lemon juice to taste

Blend sesame seed meal and water to a smooth consistency. Add oil, seasoning, and lemon juice and blend to make a thick, creamy dressing. Thin or change to suit taste. Makes 8 servings.

DR. JENSEN'S DRINK

1 tablespoon sesame seed meal   *¼ avocado*
   or butter   *1 teaspoon honey*
1 cup liquid (fruit juice,
   vegetable juice, soy milk,
   or broth and water)

Blend all ingredients for half a minute. Makes 1 serving.

NATURAL REMEDIES AND TONICS

It is best not to use a remedy for a specific condition unless your whole diet is nutritionally balanced. Eating atrocious foods and trying to find a remedy for conditions you are producing doesn't make good sense. Use my Health and Harmony Food Regimen as a guide for a nutritionally balanced diet.

Alkalinizing System

TROPICAL STORM

½ cup grapefruit sections   *¼ cup pineapple juice*
6 spinach leaves

Blend all ingredients. Makes 1 serving.

Appetite

MAUI APPETIZER

¾ cup pineapple juice   *6 dandelion leaves*

Blend all ingredients. Makes 1 serving.

Arthritis

PEACEMAKER

1 tablespoon alfalfa seeds   1 pint water

Combine ingredients in a pan and bring to a boil. Let set overnight. Strain. Makes 2 servings.

Blood Builders

CHERRY PICKUP

1 cup mixed celery, parsley,   1 cup Bing cherry juice
  and spinach   1 cup desired vegetable juice
                                         base

Blend all ingredients. Makes 2 servings.

MIXED FRUIT PICKUP

1 cup cherry, grape, or   1 tablespoon whey powder
  pineapple juice   1 egg yolk
1 dulse tablet or ¼ teaspoon
  dulse powder

Blend all ingredients. Makes 1 serving.

Body Builder

STAMINA TONIC

½ cup coconut milk   3 fresh or revived dried figs

Blend all ingredients. Makes 1 serving.

Brain and Nervous System

SERENDIPITY BLEND

*1 teaspoon each of cottage
cheese, sunflower seeds, soaked
nuts, wheat germ, and rice
bran or polishings*

1 cup papaya tea
1 egg yolk

Blend well. Take 2 to 3 teaspoons daily.

For nervous disorders, combine radish, prune juice, and rice polishings. Celery, carrot, lettuce, tomato, and prune juices can also quiet nerves.

Complexion

SOFT AS SILK

½ cup apple juice

½ cucumber

Blend all ingredients. Makes 1 serving.

SMOOTH TONIC

½ cup cucumber juice
¼ cup endive

½ cup pineapple juice

Blend all ingredients well. Makes 1 serving.

Coronary (Heart)

Any drink, such as carrot or pineapple juice with honey, can be used. Stir until honey is dissolved.

Diarrhea

Try carob powder for control. Blackberry juice is also effective.

Gastrointestinal Disorders

MIXED BLESSING

1 cup tomato juice	*1 stalk celery*
6 leaves watercress or endive	

Blend all ingredients. Use any combination of vegetables. Sieve after blending because various stomach and intestinal disorders cannot tolerate fibrous material. Drink the liquid and discard the pulp.

Carrot juice and coconut milk can be used for colitis, gastritis, and gas. An aid in ulcer conditions is egg white, beaten to a stiff froth and used as a topping on blended drinks.

Whey. Use whey in any milk or liquefied drink for intestinal management. It is high in organic sodium. It may be used plain as a drink or in combination with a wide variety of foods, especially in blended drinks.

Gland and Nerve

SUNRISE

1 cup sweet cherry juice	*1 teaspoon chlorophyll*
1 egg yolk	*2 tablespoons wheat germ*

Blend all ingredients. Makes 1 serving.

Hair (for sheen)

SUNSHINE

1 cup sweet cherry juice   *1 cup oat straw tea*

Blend all ingredients. Makes 1 serving.

Kidneys

ROCK STEADY

2 parsley tablets   *1 cup water*

Combine. Makes 1 serving.

Laxative

Drink a warm cup of herb tea first thing in the morning. Prune juice or juice from yellow fruits or vegetables will also help.

Respiratory-Catarrhal

GET-UP-AND-GO

¼ cup bell pepper, diced   *1 cup tomato juice or*
¼ cup parsley, chopped   *carrot juice*

Blend all ingredients. Makes 1 serving.

     Use foods high in vitamins A and C. Bell peppers, especially ripe ones, have a high content of vitamin C. Parsley is rich in vitamin A. Use as a base juice or as an ingredient in blended drinks.

Rheumatic

Add 1 tablespoon of dried sweet whey (goat's whey is best) per 1 cup of any juice (except citrus) for conditions involving joint pain or stiffness. Whey may be added (usually 1 tablespoon) to broths, soups, and seed and nut milk drinks.

Skin

VELVET TOUCH

½ cup pineapple juice

⅓ cucumber, chopped

2 tablespoons chopped parsley

Blend all ingredients. Makes 1 serving.

Oat straw tea and rice polishings are also good for the skin.

Vitality

ZIPPER UPPER

1 cup apple juice

1 cup celery juice

1 tablespoon wheat germ

1 tablespoon almond nut butter

1 tablespoon soy milk powder

Blend all ingredients. Makes 2 servings.

Weight Gaining

FRUIT LIFT

½ cup dried fruit, revived

1 tablespoon soy milk

1 cup pineapple juice

1 tablespoon nut or seed butter

Blend all ingredients. Makes 1 serving

Flaxseed tea (blended if you wish to use the seed), added to any blended fruit or protein drink, can also help in gaining weight.

Weight Reducing

Blended protein drinks can be made to help reduce weight. For a satisfying noon meal, try cottage cheese in soy milk or whey with apricot, peach nectar, or apple juice for flavor. Use fresh fruits in preference to dried. Fresh apples are wonderful blended, such as diced apple in pineapple juice.

Good bases are tomato, papaya, or pineapple juices. For a citrus base, blend diced grapefruit pulp (after removing the peel) or sections of orange with pulp. Also try watercress tablets blended in drinks.

Nut and seed milks (see recipes starting on page 189) are also good to use. Soy milk may be made with low-fat soy powder, available at health food stores, or gelatin whey can be used. Try the following recipes:

STRAWBERRY-SOY DRINK

1 egg yolk	*8 ounces soy milk*
4 fresh strawberries	*Honey to taste*

Blend all ingredients. Other fresh fruits or juices may be used. Makes 1 serving.

GELATIN WHEY

¼ cup cold water	*¾ cup boiling water*
2 tablespoons plain gelatin	*3 tablespoons whey powder*

Blend cold water and gelatin. Add boiling water and whey powder and blend well. Makes 1 serving.

Variations: Vanilla: Add a few drops of pure vanilla. Orange: Add 1 tablespoon orange juice and a little grated rind. Mint: Use mint tea instead of water.

Table 9.1. **Juice and Blender Combinations for Ailments**

Ailment	Combinations
Anemia	Parsley and grape juice
Asthma	Celery and papaya juice
Bed-wetting	Celery and parsley juice
Bladder	Celery and pomegranate juice
Catarrh, colds, sore throat	Watercress, apple juice with ¼ teaspoon cream of tartar
Constipation, stomach ulcers	Celery with a little sweet cream, spinach and grapefruit juice
Colds, sinus trouble	Celery and grapefruit juices (add ¼ teaspoon cream of tartar)
Diarrhea, infection	Carrot and blackberry juice
Fever, gout, arthritis	Celery and parsley juice
Gallbladder disorders	Radish, prune, black cherry, and celery juices
Glands, goiter, impotence	Celery juice, 1 teaspoon wheat germ, ½ teaspoon Nova Scotia dulse
High blood pressure	Carrot, parsley, and celery juices
Indigestion, underweight	Coconut milk, fig, parsley, and carrot juices
Insomnia, sleeplessness	Lettuce and celery juice
Kidney disorders	Celery, parsley, and asparagus juices
Liver disorders	Radish and pineapple juices
Neuralgia	Cucumber, endive, and pineapple juices

(Continued)

Table 9.1. **Continued**

Ailment	Combinations
Overweight, obesity	Beet greens, parsley, and celery juices
Poor circulation	Beet and blackberry juices
Poor memory	Celery, carrot, prune juice, and rice polishings
Poor teeth	Beet greens, parsley, celery, and green kale juices
Reducing	Parsley, grape, and pineapple juices
Rheumatism, neuritis, neuralgia	Cucumber, endive, and whey
Rickets*	Dandelion and orange juices
Scurvy, eczema	Carrot, celery, and lemon juices
Tissue cleansing	Celery, parsley, spinach, and carrot juices

*Rickets, often caused by a vitamin D deficiency, may be cured by providing cod liver oil and calcium foods such as goat's milk or cheese. If a person gets fifteen to thirty minutes of sunshine daily, the body makes its own vitamin D. Eggs, fish, and liver are the only foods containing vitamin D, unless you credit vitamin D–fortified milk. No fruits or vegetables have any vitamin D.

THE IMPORTANCE OF FIBER IN THE DIET

In the past two decades, Dr. Denis Burkitt, an English surgeon, has driven home the point that people with high-fiber diets have almost no colon cancer, diverticulosis, diabetes, ischemic heart disease, or appendicitis. While fiber (both soluble and insoluble) from fruits, vegetables, whole grains, nuts, and seeds (not from any animal sources) is not an essential nutrient to

Table 9.2. **Fiber Foods**

Food	Fiber (Grams)	Food	Fiber (Grams)
Grapefruit (½)	0.24	Watercress	0.12
Banana	0.57	Carrot (medium)	0.75
Pear	2.30	Tomato	0.57
Cantaloupe (1 cup)	0.50	Dates (10)	1.80
Fig	0.77	Green pepper	
Apricots (3)	0.64	(raw, ½ cup)	0.60
Orange	0.56	Lentil sprouts (1 cup)	2.35
Apple	1.06	Green beans (1 cup)	2.20
Kiwi	0.84	Potato (raw)	0.50
Avocado	1.20	Spinach (½ cup, raw)	0.25
		Peas (½ cup, raw)	1.70

preserve life, it is certainly needed in significant amounts to protect against malfunction, especially in the bowel. Fiber can be part of any blender drink. The adult RDI is 25 grams.

Juice is wonderful, and juices (along with herbal teas) are among the fastest ways to take care of any vitamin or mineral deficiency in the body. But the fiber in raw liquid salads and raw blender drinks is, in my opinion, also very, very important. I feel it is safe to say that very few people these days realize how much of our health, well-being, and normal functioning of the body depends upon the bowel.

Constipation clogs the bowel, slows transmission of wastes, increases risk of diverticulosis and low-grade internal infection, and pressures intestinal toxins that would normally be expelled from the body into the bloodstream.

To relieve the problem of constipation permanently requires dietary inclusion of more fiber foods every day. I urge you, for health's sake, to make high-fiber foods part of your daily diet. Table 9.2 lists some wonderful high-fiber foods to include in your daily food plan and the amount of fiber each contains.

Cellulose fiber soaks up water like a sponge and holds it, softening the stool, allowing better peristaltic movement and reducing bowel transit time. Cellulose also adheres to heavy metals and fats, carrying them off as wastes. This helps reduce blood levels of triglycerides and cholesterol and protects against toxic metals like lead and cadmium.

CHAPTER 10

CONCLUSION

I'm sure you're going to enjoy using your juicer and blender to try some or all of my special recipes, and I'm sure you're also going to enjoy the increased sense of well-being that comes when your body has everything it needs. When you make juice or combine ingredients in a blender and drink them right away, you are getting the most possible nutritional value from the fresh fruits and raw vegetables you use. Your body will express its gratitude for all those fresh nutrients with increased energy and resistance to colds, flu, and the aches and pains of getting older. I believe we are as old as we feel.

You may have heard people get all excited about the "living enzymes" they get with fresh juice. Actually, there *are* "living enzymes" in fresh juice—several thousand living enzymes in each living cell. But enzymes are protein, and when they arrive in the stomach and small intestine, they are digested like any other protein. At that point, there really is something to get excited about because when enzymes are broken down, chemical elements, such as iron, copper, and zinc, or B-complex vitamins, plus the amino acids every enzyme was made of, are released. Papaya and pineapple enzymes have been used to aid digestion.

I want to encourage you to use your blender to include high-fiber foods in your special health cocktails. Constipation is a chronic problem with millions of Americans, and it is completely unnecessary. Bananas, prunes, and peaches add lovely fiber. Sometimes I toss a handful of washed fresh parsley in the blender with a tablespoon of raw pumpkin seeds, and it does a world of good for me, providing chlorophyll, zinc, calcium, B-complex, vitamin C, and fiber.

Now, at the age of ninety-one, juices are life to me. I can get all the good out of them without any problems. Of course, I try to eat carefully, too. Always try for a balanced diet every day.

Don't forget to exercise every day. You can put all the good nutritional values you want into your body, but if your blood circulation isn't what it should be, you won't be getting all the good out of your food and drink. If you can't do anything but walk, then walk—uphill and downhill, if you can. Some of the Hunzakuts I met in Pakistan who lived to be in their 120s to 140s had never seen a doctor in their lives, and they walked along mountain trails every day. Their meals were simple, mostly vegetarian with a little meat, but the glacier water they drank was loaded with minerals. You can get the same minerals from juices.

I've enjoyed sharing with you the health-building fun of juicing. It's been a wonderful part of my life, and my hope is that it will be a wonderful part of yours.

INDEX